ROWAN

The Pure Wool Worsted Collection

A Collection of 8 designs by Martin Storey
using Pure Wool Worsted

Sandrift Scarf
pattern page 40

6

Morna
pattern page 32

Alba
pattern page 25

Spence
pattern page 43

Paisley
pattern page 37

Skerry Beret
pattern page 42

The Yarn

Pure Wool Worsted 9802170

Soft 100% superwash wool, machine washable worsted weight yarn, available in 50 lovely shades ranging from soft neutrals to mid tone brights and deep darks.

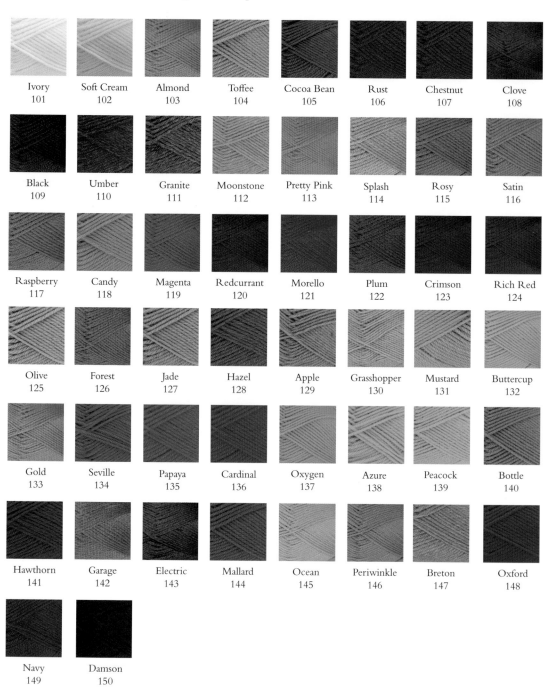

Ivory 101	Soft Cream 102	Almond 103	Toffee 104	Cocoa Bean 105	Rust 106	Chestnut 107	Clove 108
Black 109	Umber 110	Granite 111	Moonstone 112	Pretty Pink 113	Splash 114	Rosy 115	Satin 116
Raspberry 117	Candy 118	Magenta 119	Redcurrant 120	Morello 121	Plum 122	Crimson 123	Rich Red 124
Olive 125	Forest 126	Jade 127	Hazel 128	Apple 129	Grasshopper 130	Mustard 131	Buttercup 132
Gold 133	Seville 134	Papaya 135	Cardinal 136	Oxygen 137	Azure 138	Peacock 139	Bottle 140
Hawthorn 141	Garage 142	Electric 143	Mallard 144	Ocean 145	Periwinkle 146	Breton 147	Oxford 148
Navy 149	Damson 150						

Main image page 12

Alba ★ ★

SIZES

S	M	L	XL	XXL

To fit bust
81-86 91-97 102-107 112-117 122-127 cm
32-34 36-38 40-42 44-46 48-50 in

YARN

Pure Wool Worsted
6 7 8 9 10 x 100gm
(photographed in Gold 133)

NEEDLES

1 pair 4mm (no 8) (US 6) needles
1 pair 4½mm (no 7) (US 7) needles
4mm (no 8) (US 6) circular needle 60 cm long
Cable needle

TENSION

21 sts and 29 rows to 10 cm measured over patt
using 4½mm (US 7) needles.

SPECIAL ABBREVIATIONS

C3B = slip next 2 sts onto cable needle and leave at
back of work, K1, then K2 from cable needle; **C3F**
= slip next st onto cable needle and leave at front of
work, K2, then K1 from cable needle.

BACK (knitted sideways, beg at right cuff edge)
Using 4½mm (US 7) needles cast on 55 [57: 59:
61: 63] sts.
Work in patt as folls:
Row 1 (RS): K2 [6: 0: 1: 4], P2 [2: 0: 2: 2], K1, ★P2,
K6, P2, K1, rep from ★ to last 6 [4: 3: 2: 1] sts,
P2 [2: 2: 2: 1], K4 [2: 1: 0: 0].
Row 2: Purl.

Row 3: K2 [3: 0: 1: 1], (C3F) 0 [1: 0: 0: 1] times, P2
[2: 0: 2: 2], K1, ★P2, C3B, C3F, P2, K1, rep from ★ to
last 6 [4: 3: 2: 1] sts, P2 [2: 2: 2: 1], (C3B) 1 [0: 0: 0:
0] times, K1 [2: 1: 0: 0].
Row 4: Purl.
These 4 rows form patt.
Cont in patt, inc 1 st at beg (shoulder edge) of 3rd
[9th: 7th: 5th: 3rd] and 1 [0: 1: 1: 1] foll 10th row,
taking inc sts into patt. 57 [58: 61: 63: 65] sts.
Work 5 [9: 1: 3: 5] rows, ending with RS facing for
next row.
Taking all inc and cast-on sts into patt, cont as folls:
Inc 1 st at end (underarm edge) of next and foll 4th
row, then on foll alt row, then at same edge on foll 4
rows, ending with **WS** facing for next row, **and at
same time** inc 1 st at beg (shoulder edge) of
5th [next: 9th: 7th: 5th] and 0 [1: 0: 0: 0] foll 10th
row. 65 [67: 69: 71: 73] sts.
Shape side seam
Cast on 33 [35: 36: 37: 38] sts at beg of next row.
98 [102: 105: 108: 111] sts.
Inc 1 st at beg (shoulder edge) of 3rd [9th: 7th: 5th:
3rd] and 2 [2: 3: 4: 5] foll 10th rows.
101 [105: 109: 113: 117] sts.
Work 9 rows, ending with RS facing for next row.
Shape back neck
Keeping patt correct, dec 1 st at neck edge (this was
shoulder edge) of next 3 rows, then on foll alt row,
then on foll 4th row. 96 [100: 104: 108: 112] sts.
Work 51 [51: 55: 55: 59] rows, ending with RS
facing for next row.
Inc 1 st at neck edge of next and foll 4th row, then
on foll alt row, then on foll 2 rows, ending with **WS**
facing for next row. 101 [105: 109: 113: 117] sts.
Back neck shaping is now complete.

**Now shape other shoulder seam as folls:
Keeping patt correct, dec 1 st at shoulder edge (this was neck edge) of 10th and 2 [2: 3: 4: 5] foll 10th rows. 98 [102: 105: 108: 111] sts.
Work 2 [8: 6: 4: 2] rows, ending with **WS** facing for next row.

Shape side seam
Cast off 33 [35: 36: 37: 38] sts at beg of next row. 65 [67: 69: 71: 73] sts.
Dec 1 st at underarm edge of next 5 rows, then on foll alt row, then on foll 4th row **and at same time** dec 1 st at shoulder edge of 7th [next: 3rd: 5th: 7th] and 0 [1: 0: 0: 0] foll 10th row. 57 [58: 61: 63: 65] sts.
Dec 1 st at shoulder edge **only** on 6th [10th: 2nd: 4th: 6th] and 1 [0: 1: 1: 1] foll 10th row. 55 [57: 59: 61: 63] sts.
Work 5 [11: 9: 7: 5] rows, ending with RS facing for next row.
Cast off.

FRONT (knitted sideways, beg at left cuff edge)
Work as given for back to beg of back neck shaping.
Shape front neck
Keeping patt correct, cast off 8 [8: 9: 9: 10] sts at beg of next row. 93 [97: 100: 104: 107] sts.
Dec 1 st at neck edge of next 8 [8: 10: 10: 12] rows, then on foll 3 [3: 2: 2: 1] alt rows, then on 2 foll 4th rows. 80 [84: 86: 90: 92] sts.
Work 23 [23: 27: 27: 31] rows, ending with RS facing for next row.
Inc 1 st at neck edge of next and 2 foll 4th rows, then on foll 3 [3: 2: 2: 1] alt rows, then on foll 7 [7: 9: 9: 11] rows, ending with RS facing for next row. 93 [97: 100: 104: 107] sts.
Cast on 8 [8: 9: 9: 10] sts at beg of next row, ending with **WS** facing for next row. 101 [105: 109: 113: 117] sts.
Front neck shaping is now complete.
Complete to match back from **.

MAKING UP
Press as described on the information page.
Join both shoulder/overarm seams using back stitch, or mattress stitch if preferred.
Collar
With RS facing and using 4mm (US 6) circular needle, beg and ending at left shoulder seam, pick up and knit 29 [29: 30: 30: 31] sts down left side of front neck, 16 [16: 18: 18: 22] sts from front, 29 [29: 30: 30: 31] sts up right side of front neck, 8 sts down right side of back neck, 36 [36: 38: 38: 41] sts from back, and 8 sts up left side of back neck. 126 [126: 132: 132: 141] sts.
Round 1 (RS): *K2, P1, rep from * to end.
Rep this round 7 times more.
Round 9: *K2, inc purlwise in next st, rep from * to end. 168 [168: 176: 176: 188] sts.
Round 10: *K2, P2, rep from * to end.
Rep last round until collar meas 32 cm from pick-up round.
Cast off in rib.

Armhole borders (both alike)
With RS facing and using 4mm (US 6) needles, pick up and knit 110 [114: 118: 122: 126] sts evenly along cast-on/cast-off armhole opening edge.
Row 1 (WS): P2, *K2, P2, rep from * to end.
Row 2: K2, *P2, K2, rep from * to end.
These 2 rows form rib.
Work in rib for a further 11 rows, ending with RS facing for next row.
Cast off in rib.

Hem borders (both alike)
With RS facing and using 4mm (US 6) needles, pick up and knit 94 [102: 118: 130: 142] sts evenly along lower (straight row-end) edge.
Beg with row 1, work in rib as given for armhole borders for 13 cm, ending with RS facing for next row.
Cast off in rib.
See information page for finishing instructions.

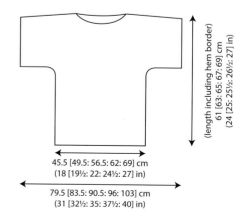

45.5 [49.5: 56.5: 62: 69] cm
(18 [19½: 22: 24½: 27] in)

79.5 [83.5: 90.5: 96: 103] cm
(31 [32½: 35: 37½: 40] in)

(length including hem border)
61 [63: 65: 67: 69] cm
(24 [25: 25½: 26½: 27] in)

Main image page 22

Kerrera ★ ★

SIZES

S	M	L	XL	XXL

To fit bust

81-86 91-97 102-107 112-117 122-127 cm
32-34 36-38 40-42 44-46 48-50 in

YARN

Pure Wool Worsted

5	6	7	7	8	x 100gm

(photographed in Satin 116)

NEEDLES

1 pair 4mm (no 8) (US 6) needles
1 pair 4½mm (no 7) (US 7) needles
Cable needle

TENSION

Based on a st st tension of 20 sts and 25 rows to 10 cm using 4½mm (US 7) needles. Body patt panel (127 sts) meas 53 cm. Sleeve patt panel (76 sts) meas 27 cm. (Over patt, 26 rows meas 10 cm.)

SPECIAL ABBREVIATIONS

C2B = slip next st onto cable needle and leave at back of work, K1, then K1 from cable needle; **C2F** = slip next st onto cable needle and leave at front of work, K1, then K1 from cable needle; **C4B** = slip next 2 sts onto cable needle and leave at back of work, K2, then K2 from cable needle; **C4F** = slip next 2 sts onto cable needle and leave at front of work, K2, then K2 from cable needle; **C7B** = slip next 4 sts onto cable needle and leave at back of work, K1 tbl, P1, K1 tbl, then (P1, K1 tbl) twice

from cable needle; **Cr3L** = slip next 2 sts onto cable needle and leave at front of work, P1, then K2 from cable needle; **Cr3R** = slip next st onto cable needle and leave at back of work, K2, then P1 from cable needle.

BACK

Using 4mm (US 6) needles cast on 114 [126: 138: 150: 162] sts.
Row 1 (RS): K2, ★P2, K2, rep from ★ to end.
Row 2: P2, ★K2, P2, rep from ★ to end.
These 2 rows form rib.
Cont in rib for a further 7 rows, ending with **WS** facing for next row.
Row 10 (WS): (Inc in first st) 1 [0: 0: 0: 1] times, rib 6 [13: 19: 25: 30], M1, (rib 5, M1) 20 times, rib 6 [13: 19: 25: 30], (inc in last st) 1 [0: 0: 0: 1] times. 137 [147: 159: 171: 185] sts.
Change to 4½mm (US 7) needles.
Now work in patt as folls:
Row 1 (RS): K1 [0: 0: 0: 1], (P1, K1) 2 [5: 8: 11: 14] times, work next 127 sts as row 1 of body patt panel, (K1, P1) 2 [5: 8: 11: 14] times, K1 [0: 0: 0: 1].
Row 2: K1 [0: 0: 0: 1], (P1, K1) 2 [5: 8: 11: 14] times, work next 127 sts as row 2 of body patt panel, (K1, P1) 2 [5: 8: 11: 14] times, K1 [0: 0: 0: 1].
These 2 rows set the sts – centre 127 sts foll chart for body patt panel with edge sts in moss st.
Working appropriate patt reps and keeping sts correct as now set, cont as folls:
Cont straight until back meas 44 [46: 48: 50: 52] cm, ending with RS facing for next row.
Shape shoulders and back neck

Next row (RS): Cast off 11 [12: 13: 15: 16] sts, patt until there are 37 [41: 45: 49: 54] sts on right needle and turn, leaving rem sts on a holder.

Work each side of neck separately.

Dec 1 st at neck edge of next 4 rows **and at same time** cast off 11 [12: 13: 15: 16] sts at beg of 2nd row, then 11 [12: 14: 15: 17] sts at beg of foll alt row.

Work 1 row.

Cast off rem 11 [13: 14: 15: 17] sts.

With RS facing, slip centre 41 [41: 43: 43: 45] sts onto a holder, rejoin yarn and patt to end.

Complete to match first side, reversing shapings.

FRONT

Work as given for back until 6 [6: 8: 8: 10] rows less have been worked than on back to beg of shoulder shaping, ending with RS facing for next row.

Shape front neck

Next row (RS): Patt 52 [57: 63: 69: 76] sts and turn, leaving rem sts on a holder.

Work each side of neck separately.

Keeping patt correct, dec 1 st at neck edge of next 5 [5: 6: 6: 6] rows, then on foll 0 [0: 0: 0: 1] alt row. 47 [52: 57: 63: 69] sts.

Work 0 [0: 1: 1: 1] row, ending with RS facing for next row.

Shape shoulder

Cast off 11 [12: 13: 15: 16] sts at beg of next and foll alt row, then 11 [12: 14: 15: 17] sts at beg of foll alt row **and at same time** dec 1 st at neck edge of next and foll 2 alt rows.

Work 1 row.

Cast off rem 11 [13: 14: 15: 17] sts.

With RS facing, slip centre 33 sts onto a holder, rejoin yarn and patt to end.

Complete to match first side, reversing shapings.

SLEEVES

Using 4mm (US 6) needles cast on 66 [70: 74: 78: 82] sts.

Work in rib as given for back for 9 rows, ending with **WS** facing for next row.

Row 10 (WS): Rib 5 [7: 9: 11: 13], (rib 1, M1, rib 3, M1, rib 1) 11 times, rib 6 [8: 10: 12: 14]. 88 [92: 96: 100: 104] sts.

Change to 4½mm (US 7) needles.

Now work in patt as folls:

Row 1 (RS): (P1, K1) 3 [4: 5: 6: 7] times, work next 76 sts as row 1 of sleeve patt panel, (K1, P1) 3 [4: 5: 6: 7] times.

Row 2: (P1, K1) 3 [4: 5: 6: 7] times, work next 76 sts as row 2 of sleeve patt panel, (K1, P1) 3 [4: 5: 6: 7] times.

These 2 rows set the sts – centre 76 sts foll chart for sleeve patt panel with edge sts in moss st.

Repeating the 16 row patt rep throughout and keeping sts correct as now set, cont as folls:

Cont straight until sleeve meas 18 [19: 20: 20: 20] cm, ending with RS facing for next row.

Cast off.

MAKING UP

Press as described on the information page.

Join right shoulder seam using back stitch, or mattress stitch if preferred.

Neckband

With RS facing and using 4mm (US 6) needles, pick up and knit 11 [11: 12: 12: 15] sts down left side of front neck, K across 33 sts on front holder, pick up and knit 11 [11: 12: 12: 15] sts up right side of front neck, and 5 sts down right side of back neck, K across 41 [41: 43: 43: 45] sts on back holder, then pick up and knit 5 sts up left side of back neck. 106 [106: 110: 110: 118] sts.

Beg with row 2, work in rib as given for back for 9 rows, ending with RS facing for next row.

Beg with a K row, work in st st for 6 rows, ending with RS facing for next row.

Cast off.

Join left shoulder and neckband seam, reversing neckband seam for st st roll.

Mark points along side seam edges 17 [18: 19: 20: 21] cm either side of shoulder seams to denote base of armhole openings. See information page for finishing instructions, setting in sleeves using the straight cast-off method.

Sleeve Chart

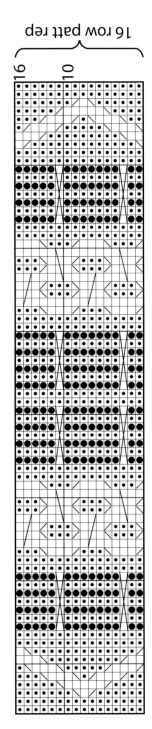

16

10

key

☐ K on RS, P on WS

⊡ P on RS, K on WS

⬤ K1tbl on RS, P1tbl on WS

▨▨ C2B

◣◣ C2F

▨▨▨ Cr3R

◣◣◣ Cr3L

▱▱▱▱ C4B

▱▱▱▱ C4F

▱▱▱▱▱▱ C7B

Body Chart

16 row patt rep

28 row patt re

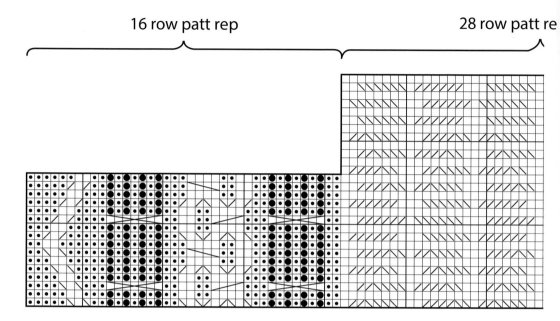

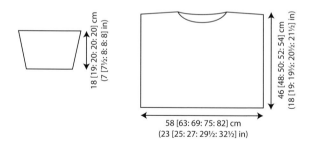

18 [19: 20: 20: 20] cm
(7 [7½: 8: 8: 8] in)

46 [48: 50: 52: 54] cm
(18 [19: 19½: 20½: 21½] in)

58 [63: 69: 75: 82] cm
(23 [25: 27: 29½: 32½] in)

16 row patt rep

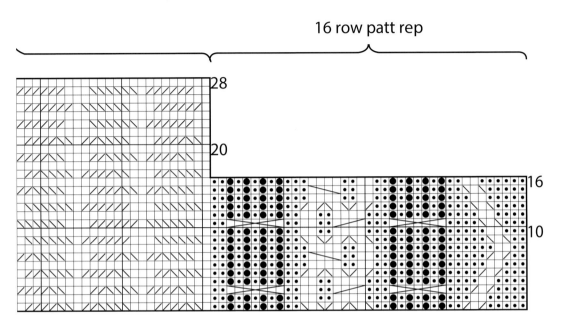

Main image page 8

Morna ★ ★ ★

SIZES

S	M	L	XL	XXL

To fit bust

81-86 91-97 102-107 112-117 122-127 cm

32-34 36-38 40-42 44-46 48-50 in

YARN

Pure Wool Worsted

9	10	11	12	13	x 100gm

(photographed in Olive 125)

NEEDLES

1 pair 4mm (no 8) (US 6) needles

1 pair 4½mm (no 7) (US 7) needles

4mm (no 8) (US 6) circular needle 150 cm long

Cable needle

BUTTONS – 4 x BN1671 from Bedecked. Please see information page for contact details.

TENSION

19 sts and 30 rows to 10 cm measured over patt using 4½mm (US 7) needles.

SPECIAL ABBREVIATIONS

C2B = slip next st onto cable needle and leave at back of work, K1, then K1 from cable needle; **C2F** = slip next st onto cable needle and leave at front of work, K1, then K1 from cable needle.

BACK

Using 4mm (US 6) needles cast on 102 [110: 122: 134: 146] sts.

Row 1 (RS): K2, ★P2, K2, rep from ★ to end.

Row 2: P2, ★K2, P2, rep from ★ to end.

These 2 rows form rib.

Cont in rib for a further 22 rows, dec 1 st at each end of last row and ending with RS facing for next row. 100 [108: 120: 132: 144] sts.

Change to 4½mm (US 7) needles.

Beg and ending rows as indicated and repeating the 24 row patt repeat throughout, cont in patt from chart as folls:

Cont straight until back meas 32 [33: 34: 35: 36] cm, ending with RS facing for next row.

Keeping patt correct, dec 1 st at each end of next and foll 10th row, then on foll 8th row, then on 4 foll 6th rows, then on 3 foll 4th rows.

80 [88: 100: 112: 124] sts.

Work 13 rows, ending with RS facing for next row.

Inc 1 st at each end of next and 2 foll 6th rows, then on 3 foll 8th rows, taking inc sts into patt.

92 [100: 112: 124: 136] sts.

Work 7 rows, ending with RS facing for next row. (Back should meas approx 69 [70: 71: 72: 73] cm.)

Shape armholes

Keeping patt correct, cast off 4 sts at beg of next 2 rows. 84 [92: 104: 116: 128] sts.

Dec 1 st at each end of next and foll 5 alt rows. 72 [80: 92: 104: 116] sts.

Cont straight until armhole meas 23 [24: 25: 26: 27] cm, ending with RS facing for next row.

Shape back neck and shoulders

Next row (RS): Cast off 4 [5: 6: 8: 9] sts, patt until there are 17 [20: 24: 28: 32] sts on right needle and turn, leaving rem sts on a holder.

Work each side of neck separately.

Dec 1 st at neck edge of next 4 rows **and at same time** cast off 4 [5: 6: 8: 9] sts at beg of 2nd row, then 4 [5: 7: 8: 9] sts at beg of foll alt row.

Work 1 row.

Cast off rem 5 [6: 7: 8: 10] sts.

With RS facing, slip centre 30 [30: 32: 32: 34] sts onto a holder, rejoin yarn and patt to end.

Complete to match first side, reversing shapings.

LEFT FRONT

Using 4mm (US 6) needles cast on 47 [51:59:63:71] sts.

Row 1 (RS): K2, *P2, K2, rep from * to last st, K1.

Row 2: K1, P2, *K2, P2, rep from * to end.

These 2 rows form rib.

Cont in rib for a further 22 rows, dec 0 [0: 1: 0: 1] at each end of last row and ending with RS facing for next row. 47 [51: 57: 63: 69] sts.

Change to 4½mm (US 7) needles.

Beg and ending rows as indicated, cont in patt from chart as folls:

Cont straight until left front meas 32 [33: 34: 35: 36] cm, ending with RS facing for next row.

Keeping patt correct, dec 1 st at beg of next and foll 10th row, then on foll 8th row, then on 4 foll 6th rows, then on 3 foll 4th rows. 37 [41: 47: 53: 59] sts.

Work 13 rows, ending with RS facing for next row.

Inc 1 st at beg of next and 2 foll 6th rows, taking inc sts into patt. 40 [44: 50: 56: 62] sts.

Work 3 rows, ending with RS facing for next row.

Shape front slope

Keeping patt correct, dec 1 st at end of next and 1 [0: 1: 0: 1] foll 4th row, then on 3 [4: 3: 4: 3] foll 6th rows **and at same time** inc 1 st at beg of 5th and 2 foll 8th rows. 38 [42: 48: 54: 60] sts.

Work 5 [3: 5: 3: 5] rows, ending with RS facing for next row.

Shape armhole

Keeping patt correct, cast off 4 sts at beg and dec 1 [0: 1: 0: 1] st at end of next row.

33 [38: 43: 50: 55] sts.

Work 1 row.

Dec 1 st at armhole edge of next and foll 5 alt rows **and at same time** dec 1 st at front slope edge of 5th [next: 5th: next: 5th] and foll 6th row.

25 [30: 35: 42: 47] sts.

Dec 1 st at front slope edge **only** on 6th [2nd: 6th: 2nd: 6th] and 7 [8: 8: 9: 9] foll 6th rows.

17 [21: 26: 32: 37] sts.

Cont straight until left front matches back to beg of shoulder shaping, ending with RS facing for next row.

Shape shoulder

Cast off 4 [5: 6: 8: 9] sts at beg of next and foll alt row, then 4 [5: 7: 8: 9] sts at beg of foll alt row.

Work 1 row.

Cast off rem 5 [6: 7: 8: 10] sts.

RIGHT FRONT

Using 4mm (US 6) needles cast on 47 [51: 59: 63: 71] sts.

Row 1 (RS): K3, *P2, K2, rep from * to end.

Row 2: P2, *K2, P2, rep from * to last st, K1.

These 2 rows form rib.

Cont in rib for a further 22 rows, dec 0 [0: 1: 0: 1] st at each end of last row and ending with RS facing for next row. 47 [51: 57: 63: 69] sts.

Change to 4½mm (US 7) needles.

Beg and ending rows as indicated, cont in patt from chart as folls:

Cont straight until right front meas 32 [33: 34: 35: 36] cm, ending with RS facing for next row.

Keeping patt correct, dec 1 st at end of next and foll 10th row, then on foll 8th row, then on 4 foll 6th rows, then on 3 foll 4th rows. 37 [41: 47: 53: 59] sts.

Complete to match left front, reversing shapings.

SLEEVES

Using 4mm (US 6) needles cast on 50 [50: 54: 54: 54] sts.

Work in rib as given for back for 18 cm, dec 1 [0: 1: 1: 0] st at each end of last row and ending with RS facing for next row. 48 [50: 52: 52: 54] sts.

Change to 4½mm (US 7) needles.

Beg and ending rows as indicated, cont in patt from chart as folls:

Inc 1 st at each end of 3rd and every foll 4th row to 68 [74: 78: 90: 98] sts, then on every foll 6th row until there are 86 [90: 94: 98: 102] sts, taking inc sts into patt.

Cont straight until sleeve meas 54 [55: 56: 56: 56] cm, ending with RS facing for next row.

Shape top

Keeping patt correct, cast off 4 sts at beg of next 2 rows. 78 [82: 86: 90: 94] sts.

Dec 1 st at each end of next and foll 4 alt rows, then on foll row, ending with RS facing for next row.

Cast off rem 66 [70: 74: 78: 82] sts.

MAKING UP

Press as described on the information page.

Join both shoulder seams using back stitch, or mattress stitch if preferred.

Front band and collar

With RS facing and using 4mm (US 6) circular needle, beg and ending at cast-on edges, pick up and knit 130 [132: 135: 137: 139] sts up right front opening edge to beg of front slope shaping, 79 [81: 83: 87: 88] sts up right front slope, and 6 sts down right side of back neck, K across 30 [30: 32: 32: 34] sts on back holder, then pick up and knit 6 sts up left side of back neck, 79 [81: 83: 87: 88] sts down left front slope to beg of front slope shaping, and 130 [132: 135: 137: 139] sts down left front opening edge. 460 [468: 480: 492: 500] sts.

Row 1 (WS): K3, ✶P2, K2, rep from ✶ to last st, K1. This row sets the sts – first and last st of every row

worked as a K st with all other sts in rib as given for back.

Keeping sts correct as now set, cont as folls:

Row 2: Rib 250 [254: 261: 267: 272], wrap next st (by slipping next st from left needle onto right needle, taking yarn to opposite side of work between needles and then slipping same st back onto left needle - when working back across wrapped sts work the wrapped st and the wrapping loop tog as one st) and turn.

Row 3: Rib 40 [40: 42: 42: 44], wrap next st and turn.

Row 4: Rib 45 [45: 47: 47: 49], wrap next st and turn.

Row 5: Rib 50 [50: 52: 52: 54], wrap next st and turn.

Row 6: Rib 55 [55: 57: 57: 59], wrap next st and turn.

Row 7: Rib 60 [60: 62: 62: 64], wrap next st and turn.

Row 8: Rib 65 [65: 67: 67: 69], wrap next st and turn.

Row 9: Rib 70 [70: 72: 72: 74], wrap next st and turn.

Row 10: Rib 75 [75: 77: 77: 80], wrap next st and

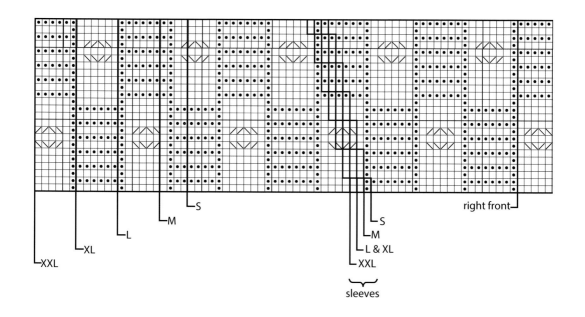

turn.

Row 11: Rib 80 [80: 82: 82: 86], wrap next st and turn.

Row 12: Rib 85 [85: 87: 88: 92], wrap next st and turn.

Row 13: Rib 90 [90: 92: 94: 98], wrap next st and turn.

Row 14: Rib 95 [95: 97: 100: 104], wrap next st and turn.

Row 15: Rib 100 [100: 102: 106: 110], wrap next st and turn.

Row 16: Rib 105 [105: 107: 112: 116], wrap next st and turn.

Row 17: Rib 110 [110: 112: 118: 122], wrap next st and turn.

Row 18: Rib 115 [115: 117: 124: 128], wrap next st and turn.

Row 19: Rib 120 [120: 122: 130: 134], wrap next st and turn.

Row 20: Rib 125 [125: 128: 136: 140], wrap next st and turn.

Row 21: Rib 130 [130: 134: 142: 146], wrap next st and turn.

Row 22: Rib 135 [135: 140: 148: 152], wrap next st and turn.

Row 23: Rib 140 [140: 146: 154: 158], wrap next st and turn.

Row 24: Rib 145 [146: 152: 160: 164], wrap next st and turn.

Row 25: Rib 150 [152: 158: 166: 170], wrap next st and turn.

Row 26: Rib 155 [158: 164: 172: 176], wrap next st and turn.

Row 27: Rib 160 [164: 170: 178: 182], wrap next st and turn.

Row 28: Rib 166 [170: 176: 184: 188], wrap next st and turn.

Row 29: Rib 172 [176: 182: 190: 194], wrap next st and turn.

Row 30: Rib 178 [182: 188: 196: 200], wrap next st and turn.

Row 31: Rib 184 [188: 194: 202: 206], wrap next st and turn.

Row 32: Rib 190 [194: 200: 208: 212], wrap next st and turn.

Row 33: Rib 196 [200: 206: 214: 218], wrap next st and turn.

Row 34: Rib to end.

Now working across **all** sts, cont as folls:

Work 5 rows, ending with RS facing for next row.

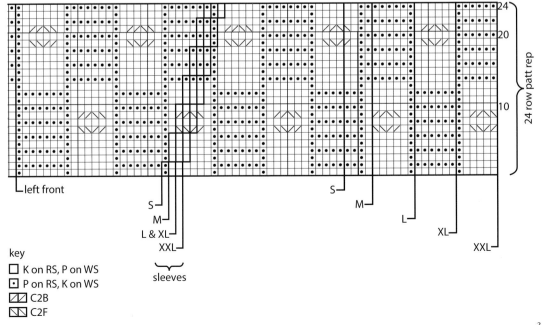

key
☐ K on RS, P on WS
⊡ P on RS, K on WS
▨ C2B
▧ C2F

sleeves

Next row (RS): Rib 42 [44: 44: 43: 42], ★cast off 2 sts (to make a buttonhole – cast on 2 sts over these cast-off sts on next row), rib until there are 26 [26: 27: 28: 29] sts on right needle after cast-off, rep from ★ twice more, cast off 2 sts (to make 4th buttonhole – cast on 2 sts over these cast-off sts on next row), rib to end.

Work a further 7 rows, ending with RS facing for next row.

Cast off in rib.

Pockets (make 2)

Using 4½mm (US 7) needles cast on 36 sts.

Work in patt as folls:

Row 1 (RS): K7, (P1, K6) 4 times, K1.

Row 2: K1, (P6, K8) twice, P6, K1.

Rows 3 to 6: As rows 1 and 2, twice.

Row 7: K1, (K1, C2B, C2F, K1, P1, K6, P1) twice, K1, C2B, C2F, K2.

Row 8: As row 2.

Row 9: K1, (K1, C2F, C2B, K1, P1, K6, P1) twice, K1, C2F, C2B, K2.

Row 10: As row 2.

Rows 11 and 12: As rows 1 and 2.

Row 13: K7, (P1, K6) 4 times, K1.

Row 14: (K8, P6) twice, K8.

Rows 15 to 18: As rows 13 and 14, twice.

Row 19: K1, (K6, P1, K1, C2B, C2F, K1, P1) twice, K7.

Row 20: As row 14.

Row 21: K1, (K6, P1, K1, C2F, C2B, K1, P1) twice, K7.

Row 22: As row 14.

Rows 23 and 24: As rows 13 and 14.

These 24 rows form patt.

Cont in patt for a further 24 rows, ending with RS facing for next row.

Change to 4mm (US 6) needles.

Next row (RS): K3, ★P2, K2, rep from ★ to last st, K1.

Next row: K1, P2, ★K2, P2, rep from ★ to last st, K1.

Rep last 2 rows 3 times more, ending with RS facing for next row.

Cast off in rib.

See information page for finishing instructions, setting in sleeves using the shallow set-in method and reversing sleeve seam for first 12 cm. Fold first 9 cm of cuff to RS (to form turn-back) and secure in place at sleeve seam. Using photograph as a guide and ensuring patt on pocket and fronts match, sew pockets onto fronts.

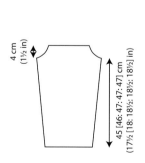

4 cm
(1½ in)

45 [46: 47: 47: 47] cm
(17½ [18: 18½: 18½: 18½] in)

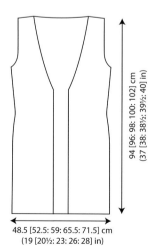

94 [96: 98: 100: 102] cm
(37 [38: 38½: 39½: 40] in)

48.5 [52.5: 59: 65.5: 71.5] cm
(19 [20½: 23: 26: 28] in)

Main image page 18

Paisley ★ ★

SIZES

S	M	L	XL	XXL

To fit bust

81-86 91-97 102-107 112-117 122-127 cm

32-34 36-38 40-42 44-46 48-50 in

YARN

Pure Wool Worsted

7 7 8 9 9 x 100gm

(photographed in Grasshopper 130)

NEEDLES

1 pair 4mm (no 8) (US 6) needles

1 pair 4½mm (no 7) (US 7) needles

Cable needle

TENSION

20 sts and 25 rows to 10 cm measured over st st using 4½mm (US 7) needles. Cable panel (56 sts) meas 18 cm.

SPECIAL ABBREVIATIONS

C6B = slip next 3 sts onto cable needle and leave at back of work, K3, then K3 from cable needle; **C6F** = slip next 3 sts onto cable needle and leave at front of work, K3, then K3 from cable needle; **Cr4L** = slip next 3 sts onto cable needle and leave at front of work, P1, then K3 from cable needle; **Cr4R** = slip next st onto cable needle and leave at back of work, K3, then P1 from cable needle.

BACK

Using 4mm (US 6) needles cast on 98 [110: 122:

134: 146] sts.

Row 1 (RS): K2, ★P2, K2, rep from ★ to end.

Row 2: P2, ★K2, P2, rep from ★ to end.

These 2 rows form rib.

Work in rib for a further 30 rows, inc 1 [0: 0: 0: 1] st at each end of last row and ending with RS facing for next row. 100 [110: 122: 134: 148] sts.

Change to 4½mm (US 7) needles.

Beg with a K row, now work in st st as folls:

Cont straight until back meas 36 [37: 38: 39: 40] cm, ending with RS facing for next row.

Shape raglan armholes

Cast off 3 sts at beg of next 2 rows.

94 [104: 116: 128: 142] sts.

Next row (RS): K1, sl 1, K1, psso, K to last 3 sts, K2tog, K1.

Next row: (P1, P2tog) 0 [1: 1: 1: 1] times, P to last 0 [3: 3: 3: 3] sts, (P2tog tbl, P1) 0 [1: 1: 1: 1] times. 92 [100: 112: 124: 138] sts.

Working all raglan armhole decreases as set by last 2 rows, dec 1 st at each end of next 1 [5: 13: 23: 33] rows, then on foll 28 [28: 25: 21: 17] alt rows. 34 [34: 36: 36: 38] sts.

Work 1 row, ending with RS facing for next row. Break yarn and leave sts on a holder.

FRONT

Using 4mm (US 6) needles cast on 98 [110: 122: 134: 146] sts.

Work in rib as given for back for 31 rows, ending with **WS** facing for next row.

Row 32 (WS): (Inc in first st) 1 [0: 0: 0: 1] times, rib 29 [36: 42: 48: 53], M1, (rib 2, M1) 19 times, rib

29 [36: 42: 48: 53], (inc in last st) 1 [0: 0: 0: 1] times. 120 [130: 142: 154: 168] sts.

Change to 4½mm (US 7) needles.

Now work in patt as folls:

Row 1 (RS): K32 [37: 43: 49: 56], work next 56 sts as row 1 of cable panel, K32 [37: 43: 49: 56].

Row 2: P32 [37: 43: 49: 56], work next 56 sts as row 2 of cable panel, P32 [37: 43: 49: 56].

These 2 rows set the sts – central cable panel with st st at each side.

Keeping sts correct as now set, cont as folls:

Cont straight until front matches back to beg of raglan armhole shaping, ending with RS facing for next row.

Shape raglan armholes

Keeping patt correct, cast off 3 sts at beg of next 2 rows. 114 [124: 136: 148: 162] sts.

Working all raglan armhole decreases as set by back, dec 1 st at each end of next 1 [7: 15: 25: 35] rows, then on foll 20 [19: 15: 11: 6] alt rows. 72 [72: 76: 76: 80] sts.

Work 1 row, ending with RS facing for next row.

Shape front neck

Next row (RS): K1, sl 1, K1, psso, patt 15 [15: 17: 17: 19] sts and turn, leaving rem sts on a holder. 17 [17: 19: 19: 21] sts.

Work each side of neck separately.

Keeping patt correct, dec 1 st at neck edge of next 9 [9: 10: 10: 10] rows, then on foll 0 [0: 0: 0: 1] alt row **and at same time** dec 1 st at raglan armhole edge of 2nd and foll 3 [3: 4: 4: 5] alt rows. 4 sts.

Work 0 [0: 1: 1: 1] row, ending with RS facing for next row.

Next row (RS): K1, sl 1, K2tog, psso.

Next row: P2.

Next row: K2tog and fasten off.

With RS facing, slip centre 36 sts onto a holder, rejoin yarn and patt to last 3 sts, K2tog, K1. 17 [17: 19: 19: 21] sts.

Complete to match first side, reversing shapings.

SLEEVES

Using 4mm (US 6) needles cast on 48 [50: 52: 52: 54] sts.

Row 1 (RS): P1 [0: 1: 1: 0], K2, *P2, K2, rep from * to last 1 [0: 1: 1: 0] st, P1 [0: 1: 1: 0].

Row 2: K1 [0: 1: 1: 0], P2, *K2, P2, rep from * to last 1 [0: 1: 1: 0] st, K1 [0: 1: 1: 0].

These 2 rows form rib.

Cont in rib, inc 1 st at each end of 5th [5th: 5th: 3rd: 3rd] and 4 foll 6th rows, taking inc sts into rib. 58 [60: 62: 62: 64] sts.

Work 1 [1: 1: 3: 3] rows, ending with RS facing for next row. (32 rows of rib completed.)

Change to 4½mm (US 7) needles.

Beg with a K row, cont in st st, shaping sides by inc 1 st at each end of 5th [5th: 5th: 3rd: 3rd] and every foll 6th row until there are 76 [84: 82: 88: 90] sts, then on 2 [0: 2: 0: 0] foll 8th rows. 80 [84: 86: 88: 90] sts.

Cont straight until sleeve meas 45 [46: 47: 47: 47] cm, ending with RS facing for next row.

Shape raglan

Cast off 3 sts at beg of next 2 rows. 74 [78: 80: 82: 84] sts.

Working all raglan decreases in same way as back raglan armhole decreases, dec 1 st at each end of next 7 rows, then on every foll alt row until 14 sts rem.

Work 1 row, ending with RS facing for next row.

Left sleeve only

Dec 1 st at each end of next row, then cast off 3 sts at beg of foll row. 9 sts.

Dec 1 st at beg of next row, then cast off 2 sts at beg of foll row. 6 sts.

Right sleeve only

Cast off 4 sts at beg and dec 1 st at end of next row. 9 sts.

Work 1 row.

Cast off 2 sts at beg and dec 1 st at end of next row. 6 sts.

Work 1 row.

Both sleeves

Rep last 2 rows once more.

Cast off rem 3 sts.

MAKING UP

Press as described on the information page.

Join both front and right back raglan seams using back stitch, or mattress stitch if preferred.

Collar

With RS facing and using 4mm (US 6) needles,

pick up and knit 8 sts from top of left sleeve, and 10 [10: 12: 12: 14] sts down left side of front neck, K across 36 sts on front holder as folls: (K1, K2tog) 6 times, (K2tog tbl, K1) 6 times, pick up and knit 10 [10: 12: 12: 14] sts up right side of front neck, and 8 sts from top of right sleeve, then K across 34 [34: 36: 36: 38] sts on back holder, inc 1 st at centre. 95 [95: 101: 101: 107] sts.

Row 1 (WS): P2, *K1, P2, rep from * to end.

Row 2: K2, *P1, K2, rep from * to end.
Rep last 2 rows 3 times more.

Row 9: P2, *inc in next st, P2, rep from * to end. 126 [126: 134: 134: 142] sts.

Beg with row 1, now work in rib as given for back until collar meas 30 cm from pick-up row, ending with **WS** of body (RS of collar) facing for next row. Cast off in rib.

See information page for finishing instructions.

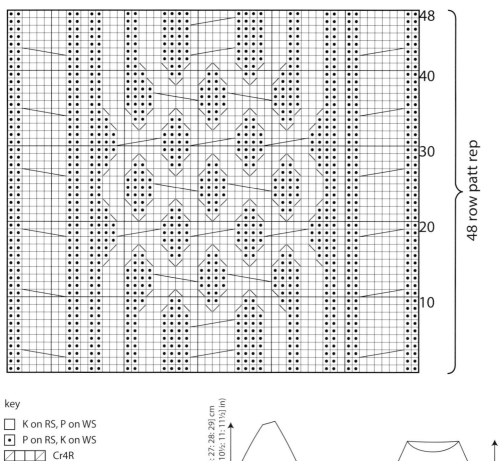

48 row patt rep

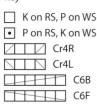

key

☐ K on RS, P on WS
• P on RS, K on WS
Cr4R
Cr4L
C6B
C6F

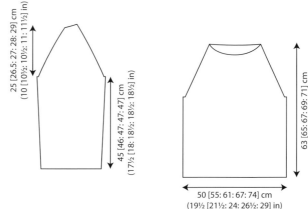

25 [26.5: 27: 28: 29] cm
(10 [10½: 10½: 11: 11½] in)

45 [46: 47: 47: 47] cm
(17½ [18: 18½: 18½: 18½] in)

63 [65: 67: 69: 71] cm
(25 [25½: 26½: 27: 28] in)

50 [55: 61: 67: 74] cm
(19½ [21½: 24: 26½: 29] in)

Main image page 6

Sandrift Scarf ★ ★

YARN

Pure Wool Worsted

A	Umber	110	3	x 100gm
B	Granite	111	3	x 100gm
C	Moonstone	112	3	x 100gm

NEEDLES

1 pair 4½mm (no 7) (US 7) needles
Cable needle

TENSION

28 ½ sts and 24 rows to 10 cm measured over patt using 4 ½mm (US 7) needles.

FINISHED SIZE

Completed scarf is 42 cm (16½ in) wide and 200 cm (78½ in) long.

SPECIAL ABBREVIATIONS

C6B = slip next 3 sts onto cable needle and leave at back of work, K3, then K3 from cable needle; **C6F** = slip next 3 sts onto cable needle and leave at front of work, K3, then K3 from cable needle; **Cr5L** = slip next 3 sts onto cable needle and leave at front of work, P2, then K3 from cable needle; **Cr5R** = slip next 2 sts onto cable needle and leave at back of work, K3, then P2 from cable needle; **Tw2L** = K into back of 2nd st on left needle, then K tog tbl first 2 sts on left needle and slip both sts off left needle at same time; **Tw2R** = K2tog leaving sts on left needle, K first of these 2 sts again and slip both sts off left needle at same time.

SCARF

Using 4½mm (US 7) needles cast on as folls: using yarn A cast on 31 sts, using yarn B cast on 31 sts, using yarn C cast on 31 sts. 93 sts.

Using the **intarsia** technique as described on the information page, work in vertical stripes as folls:

Row 1 (RS): Using yarn C K1, P1, ★Tw2R, K1, P2, (inc once in each of next 3 sts, P4) twice, inc once in each of next 3 sts, P2, Tw2R, K1★, P2, using yarn B P2, rep from ★ to ★ once more, P2, using yarn A P2, rep from ★ to ★ once more, P1, K1. 120 sts.

Row 2: Using yarn A K2, ★P3, K2, (P6, K4) twice, P6, K2, P3★, K2, using yarn B K2, rep from ★ to ★ once more, K2, using yarn C K2, rep from ★ to ★ once more, K2.

Row 3: Using yarn C K1, P1, ★K1, Tw2L, P2, (K6, P4) twice, K6, P2, K1, Tw2L★, P2, using yarn B P2, rep from ★ to ★ once more, P2, using yarn A P2, rep from ★ to ★ once more, P1, K1.

Row 4: As row 2.

These 4 rows set colour positions and form patt over edge 5 sts of each colour section.

Keeping colours and patt correct as now set, cont in main cable patt as folls:

Row 1 (RS): Patt 5 sts, ★P2, (C6B, P4) twice, C6B, P2★, patt 10 sts, rep from ★ to ★ once more, patt 10 sts, rep from ★ to ★ once more, patt 5 sts.

Row 2: Patt 5 sts, ★K2, (P6, K4) twice, P6, K2★, patt 10 sts, rep from ★ to ★ once more, patt 10 sts, rep from ★ to ★ once more, patt 5 sts.

Row 3: Patt 5 sts, ★P2, (K6, P4) twice, K6, P2★, patt 10 sts, rep from ★ to ★ once more, patt 10 sts, rep from ★ to ★ once more, patt 5 sts.

Row 4: As row 2.

Rows 5 to 8: As rows 1 to 4.

Rows 9 and 10: As rows 1 and 2.

Row 11: Patt 5 sts, *P2, K3, Cr5L, P2, K6, P2, Cr5R, K3, P2*, patt 10 sts, rep from * to * once more, patt 10 sts, rep from * to * once more, patt 5 sts.

Row 12: Patt 5 sts, *(K2, P3) twice, K2, P6, K2, (P3, K2) twice*, patt 10 sts, rep from * to * once more, patt 10 sts, rep from * to * once more, patt 5 sts.

Row 13: Patt 5 sts, *P2, (Cr5L) twice, K6, (Cr5R) twice, P2*, patt 10 sts, rep from * to * once more, patt 10 sts, rep from * to * once more, patt 5 sts.

Row 14: Patt 5 sts, *K4, P3, K2, P12, K2, P3, K4*, patt 10 sts, rep from * to * once more, patt 10 sts, rep from * to * once more, patt 5 sts.

Row 15: Patt 5 sts, *P4, Cr5L, (C6F) twice, Cr5R, P4*, patt 10 sts, rep from * to * once more, patt 10 sts, rep from * to * once more, patt 5 sts.

Row 16: Patt 5 sts, *K6, P18, K6*, patt 10 sts, rep from * to * once more, patt 10 sts, rep from * to * once more, patt 5 sts.

Row 17: Patt 5 sts, *P6, (C6B) 3 times, P6*, patt 10 sts, rep from * to * once more, patt 10 sts, rep from * to * once more, patt 5 sts.

Row 18: As row 16.

Row 19: Patt 5 sts, *P4, Cr5R, (C6F) twice, Cr5L, P4*, patt 10 sts, rep from * to * once more, patt 10 sts, rep from * to * once more, patt 5 sts.

Row 20: As row 14.

Row 21: Patt 5 sts, *P2, (Cr5R) twice, K6, (Cr5L) twice, P2*, patt 10 sts, rep from * to * once more, patt 10 sts, rep from * to * once more, patt 5 sts.

Row 22: As row 12.

Row 23: Patt 5 sts, *P2, K3, Cr5R, P2, K6, P2, Cr5L, K3, P2*, patt 10 sts, rep from * to * once more, patt 10 sts, rep from * to * once more, patt 5 sts.

Row 24: As row 2.

These 24 rows form patt.

Cont in patt until scarf meas approx 198 cm, ending after patt row 10 and with RS facing for next row. Now rep patt rows 3 and 4 once more, then patt row 3 again, ending with **WS** facing for next row.

Next row (WS): Patt 5 sts, *K2, (P2tog) 3 times, K4, (P2tog) 3 times, K4, (P2tog) 3 times, K2*, patt 10 sts, rep from * to * once more, patt 10 sts, rep from * to * once more, patt 5 sts.

Cast off rem 93 sts, using colours as set by previous row.

MAKING UP

Press as described on the information page.

Main image page 20

Skerry Beret ★

YARN
Pure Wool Worsted
       1   x 100gm
(photographed in Morello 121)

NEEDLES
1 pair 4mm (no 8) (US 6) needles
1 pair 4½mm (no 7) (US 7) needles

TENSION
20 sts and 25 rows to 10 cm measured over st st using 4½mm (US 7) needles.

BERET
Using 4mm (US 6) needles cast on 101 sts.
Row 1 (RS): K1, ★P1, K1, rep from ★ to end.
Row 2: P1, ★K1, P1, rep from ★ to end.
These 2 rows form rib.
Work in rib for a further 6 rows, ending with RS facing for next row.
Change to 4½mm (US 7) needles.
Now shape top as folls:
Row 1 (RS): (K10, M1) 10 times, K1. 111 sts.
Row 2 and every foll alt row: Purl.
Row 3: (K11, M1) 10 times, K1. 121 sts.
Row 5: (K12, M1) 10 times, K1. 131 sts.
Row 7: (K13, M1) 10 times, K1. 141 sts.
Row 9: (K14, M1) 10 times, K1. 151 sts.
Row 11: (K15, M1) 10 times, K1. 161 sts.
Row 13: (K16, M1) 10 times, K1. 171 sts.
Row 15: (K17, M1) 10 times, K1. 181 sts.
Row 17: Knit.
Row 19: Knit.

Row 21: (K16, K2tog) 10 times, K1. 171 sts.
Row 23: (K15, K2tog) 10 times, K1. 161 sts.
Row 25: (K14, K2tog) 10 times, K1. 151 sts.
Row 27: (K13, K2tog) 10 times, K1. 141 sts.
Row 29: (K12, K2tog) 10 times, K1. 131 sts.
Row 31: (K11, K2tog) 10 times, K1. 121 sts.
Row 33: (K10, K2tog) 10 times, K1. 111 sts.
Row 35: (K9, K2tog) 10 times, K1. 101 sts.
Row 37: (K8, K2tog) 10 times, K1. 91 sts.
Row 39: (K7, K2tog) 10 times, K1. 81 sts.
Row 41: (K6, K2tog) 10 times, K1. 71 sts.
Row 43: (K5, K2tog) 10 times, K1. 61 sts.
Row 45: (K4, K2tog) 10 times, K1. 51 sts.
Row 47: (K3, K2tog) 10 times, K1. 41 sts.
Row 49: (K2, K2tog) 10 times, K1. 31 sts.
Row 51: (K1, K2tog) 10 times, K1. 21 sts.
Row 53: (K2tog) 10 times, K1.
Break yarn and thread through rem 11 sts. Pull up tight and fasten off securely.

MAKING UP
Press as described on the information page.
Join back seam.
Trim
Using 4mm (US 6) needles cast on 4 sts.
Cast off knitwise.
Attach one end of trim to top of beret.

Mens main image page 14
Womens main image page 16
(woman wearing size M with sleeves rolled back for loose fit)

SIZES

XS S M L XL XXL 2XL

To fit chest

| 97 | 102 | 107 | 112 | 117 | 122 | 127 | cm |
| 38 | 40 | 42 | 44 | 46 | 48 | 50 | in |

YARN

Pure Wool Worsted

8 8 9 10 11 11 12 x 100gm

(photographed in Soft Cream 102)

NEEDLES

1 pair 4mm (no 8) (US 6) needles
1 pair 4½mm (no 7) (US 7) needles
Cable needle

TENSION

25 sts and 26 rows to 10 cm measured over patt using 4½mm (US 7) needles.

SPECIAL ABBREVIATIONS

C3F = slip next st onto cable needle and leave at front of work, K1 tbl, P1, then K1 tbl from cable needle; **C4F** = slip next 3 sts onto cable needle and leave at front of work, K1, then K3 from cable needle; **C6B** = slip next 3 sts onto cable needle and leave at back of work, K3, then K3 from cable needle; **C6F** = slip next 3 sts onto cable needle and leave at front of work, K3, then K3 from cable needle; **Cr2L** = slip next st onto cable needle and leave at front of work, P1, then K1 tbl from cable needle; **Cr2R** = slip next st onto cable needle and leave at back of work, K1 tbl, then P1 from cable needle; **Cr4L** = slip next 3 sts onto cable needle and leave at front of

work, P1, then K3 from cable needle; **Cr4R** = slip next st onto cable needle and leave at back of work, K3, then P1 from cable needle.

BACK

Using 4mm (US 6) needles cast on 129 [137: 145: 153: 169: 177: 185] sts.

Row 1 (RS): K2, ★P1, (K1 tbl, P1) twice, K3, rep from ★ to last 7 sts, P1, (K1 tbl, P1) twice, K2.

Row 2: P2, ★K1, (P1 tbl, K1) twice, P3, rep from ★ to last 7 sts, K1, (P1 tbl, K1) twice, P2.

Rows 3 and 4: As rows 1 and 2.

Row 5: K2, ★P1, C3F, P1, K3, rep from ★ to last 7 sts, P1, C3F, P1, K2.

Row 6: As row 2.

Rows 7 and 8: As rows 1 and 2.

These 8 rows form fancy rib.

Cont in fancy rib for a further 33 rows, ending with **WS** facing for next row.

Row 42 (WS): Rib 10 [14: 14: 14: 84: 88: 92], M1, (rib 18 [27: 29: 31: -: -: -], M1) 6 [4: 4: 4: 0: 0: 0] times, rib 11 [15: 15: 15: 85: 89: 93].

136 [142: 150: 158: 170: 178: 186] sts.

Change to 4½mm (US 7) needles.

Beg and ending rows as indicated, repeating the 16 and 24 row patt repeats throughout and repeating each side 19 st patt panel 2 [2: 3: 3: 3: 3: 4] times, cont in patt from chart for appropriate size of body as folls:

Cont in patt until back meas 60 [63: 66: 66: 68: 68: 71] cm, ending with RS facing for next row.

Shape shoulders and back neck

Next row (RS): Cast off 11 [11: 12: 13: 15: 15: 16] sts, patt until there are 38 [40: 43:

Spence ★ ★ ★

45: 49: 52: 55] sts on right needle and turn, leaving rem sts on a holder.

Work each side of neck separately.

Keeping patt correct, dec 1 st at neck edge of next 4 rows **and at same time** cast off 11 [12: 13: 13: 15: 16: 17] sts at beg of 2nd row, then 11 [12: 13: 14: 15: 16: 17] sts at beg of foll alt row.

Work 1 row.

Cast off rem 12 [12: 13: 14: 15: 16: 17] sts.

With RS facing, slip centre 38 [40: 40: 42: 42: 44: 44] sts onto a holder, rejoin yarn and patt to end.

Complete to match first side, reversing shapings.

FRONT

Work as given for back until 18 [18: 18: 20: 20: 22: 22] rows less have been worked than on back to beg of shoulder shaping, ending with RS facing for next row.

Shape front neck

Next row (RS): Patt 55 [57: 61: 65: 71: 75: 79] sts and turn, leaving rem sts on a holder.

Work each side of neck separately.

Keeping patt correct, dec 1 st at neck edge of next 6 rows, then on foll 3 [3: 3: 4: 4: 5: 5] alt rows, then on foll 4th row. 45 [47: 51: 54: 60: 63: 67] sts.

Work 1 row, ending with RS facing for next row.

Shape shoulder

Cast off 11 [11: 12: 13: 15: 15: 16] sts at beg of next and foll 2 [0: 0: 1: 2: 0: 0] alt rows, then − [12: 13: 14: −: 16: 17] sts at beg of foll − [2: 2: 1: −: 2: 2] alt rows.

Work 1 row.

Cast off rem 12 [12: 13: 14: 15: 16: 17] sts.

With RS facing, slip centre 26 [28: 28: 28: 28: 28: 28] sts onto a holder, rejoin yarn and patt to end.

Complete to match first side, reversing shapings.

SLEEVES

Using 4mm (US 6) needles cast on 55 [57: 59: 59: 61: 61: 65] sts.

Row 1 (RS): P0 [0: 0: 0: 1: 1: 1], (K1 tbl, P1) 0 [0: 0: 0: 0: 0: 1] times, K1 [2: 3: 3: 3: 3: 3], *P1, (K1 tbl, P1) twice, K3, rep from * to last 6 [7: 0: 0: 1: 1: 3] sts, (P1, K1 tbl) 2 [2: 0: 0: 0: 0: 1] times, P1 [1: 0: 0: 1: 1: 1], K1 [2: 0: 0: 0: 0: 0].

Row 2: K0 [0: 0: 0: 1: 1: 1], (P1 tbl, K1) 0 [0: 0: 0: 0: 0: 1] times, P1 [2: 3: 3: 3: 3: 3], *K1, (P1 tbl, K1) twice, P3, rep from * to last 6 [7: 0: 0: 1: 1: 3] sts, (K1, P1 tbl) 2 [2: 0: 0: 0: 0: 1] times, K1 [1: 0: 0: 1: 1: 1],

44

P1 [2: 0: 0: 0: 0: 0].

Rows 3 and 4: As rows 1 and 2.

Row 5: P0 [0: 0: 0: 1: 1: 1], (K1 tbl, P1) 0 [0: 0: 0: 0: 0: 1] times, K1 [2: 3: 3: 3: 3: 3], *P1, C3F, P1, K3, rep from * to last 6 [7: 0: 0: 1: 1: 3] sts, (P1, C3F) 1 [1: 0: 0: 0: 0: 0] times, (P1, K1 tbl) 0 [0: 0: 0: 0: 0: 1] times, P1 [1: 0: 0: 1: 1: 1], K1 [2: 0: 0: 0: 0: 0].

Row 6: As row 2.

Rows 7 and 8: As rows 1 and 2.

These 8 rows form fancy rib.

Cont in fancy rib for a further 14 rows, inc 1 st at centre of last row and ending with RS facing for next row. 56 [58: 60: 60: 62: 62: 66] sts.

Change to 4½mm (US 7) needles.

Beg and ending rows as indicated and repeating the 16 row patt repeat throughout, cont in patt from chart for sleeves as folls:

Inc 1 st at each end of next and foll 5 [9: 11: 18: 25: 29: 30] alt rows, then on every foll 4th row until there are 104 [114: 120: 130: 140: 144: 150] sts, taking inc sts into patt.

Cont straight until sleeve meas 45 [48: 50: 52: 53: 53: 54] cm, ending with RS facing for next row.

Cast off in patt.

MAKING UP

Press as described on the information page.

Join right shoulder seam using back stitch, or mattress stitch if preferred.

Neckband

With RS facing and using 4mm (US 6) needles, pick up and knit 19 [18: 18: 20: 20: 23: 23] sts down left side of front neck, K across 26 [28: 28: 28: 28: 28: 28] sts on front holder, pick up and knit 19 [18: 18: 20: 20: 23: 23] sts up right side of front neck, and 5 sts down right side of back neck, K across 38 [40: 40: 42: 42: 44: 44] sts on back holder inc [dec: dec: inc: inc: inc: inc] 1 st at centre, then pick up and knit 5 sts up left side of back neck. 113 [113: 113: 121: 121: 129: 129] sts.

Beg with row 2, work in fancy rib as given for back for 23 rows, ending with RS of collar facing for next row.

Cast off in patt.

Join left shoulder and neckband seam. Mark points along side seam edges 21 [23: 24: 26: 28: 29: 30] cm either side of shoulder seams (to denote base of armhole openings). See information page for finishing instructions, setting in sleeves using the straight cast-off method.

Sleeve Chart

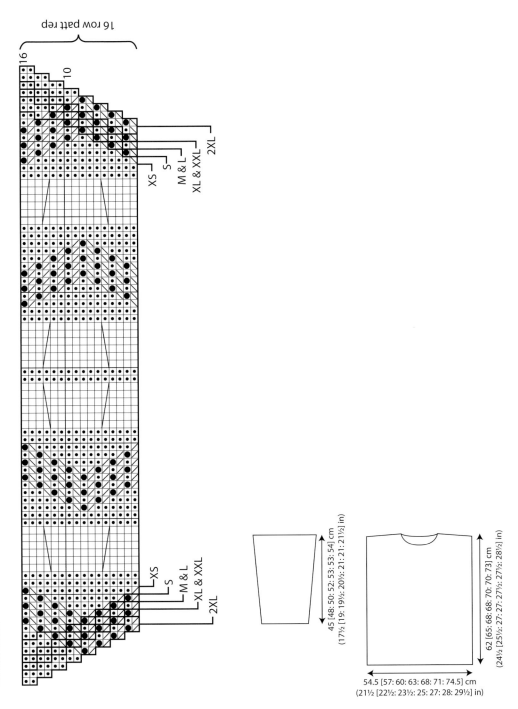

16 row patt rep

16
10

XS
S
M & L
XL & XXL
2XL

XS
S
M & L
XL & XXL
2XL

45 [48: 50: 52: 53: 53: 54] cm
(17½ [19: 19½: 20½: 21: 21: 21½] in)

62 [65: 68: 68: 70: 70: 73] cm
(24½ [25½: 27: 27: 27½: 27½: 28½] in)

54.5 [57: 60: 63: 68: 71: 74.5] cm
(21½ [22½: 23½: 25: 27: 28: 29½] in)

Sizes XS, S, XL and XXL
Body Chart

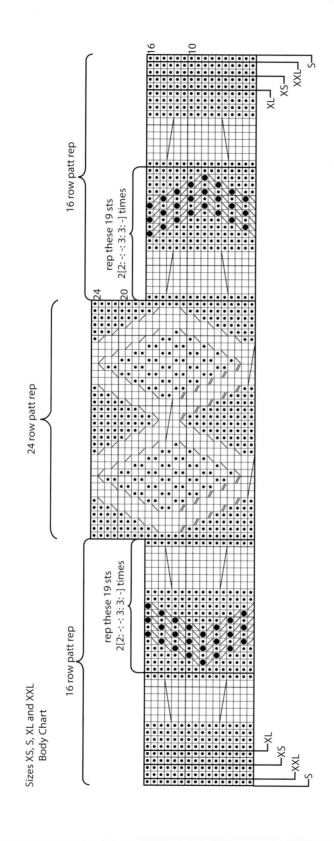

16 row patt rep

rep these 19 sts
2[2: -: -: 3: 3: -] times

24 row patt rep

rep these 19 sts
2[2: -: -: 3: 3: -] times

16 row patt rep

16

10

XL

XS

XXL

S

24

20

Sizes M, L and 2XL
Body Chart

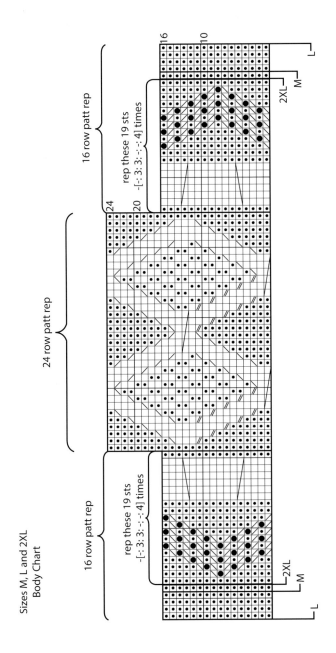

16 row patt rep

rep these 19 sts
-[-: 3: 3: -: -: 4] times

24 row patt rep

16 row patt rep

rep these 19 sts
-[-: 3: 3: -: -: 4] times

Mens main image page 11
Womens main image page 4

Tulloch ★ ★

SIZES

XXS XS S M L XL XXL 2XL
To fit bust/chest

| 91 | 97 | 102 | 107 | 112 | 117 | 122 | 127 | cm |
| 36 | 38 | 40 | 42 | 44 | 46 | 48 | 50 | in |

YARN

Pure Wool Worsted

6   6   7   8   8   9   9   10   x 100gm
(lady's photographed in Periwinkle 146, man's in
Almond 103)

NEEDLES

1 pair 4mm (no 8) (US 6) needles
1 pair 4½mm (no 7) (US 7) needles
Cable needle

BUTTONS – 10 x BN1595 (man's) or
10 x BN1709 (lady's) from Bedecked. Please see
information page for contact details.

TENSION

20 sts and 25 rows to 10 cm measured over st st
using 4½mm (US 7) needles.

SPECIAL ABBREVIATIONS

C4B = slip next 2 sts onto cable needle and leave at
back of work, K2, then K2 from cable needle; **C4F**
= slip next 2 sts onto cable needle and leave at front
of work, K2, then K2 from cable needle.

Pattern note: Buttonholes along front opening
edge are made on WS rows as well as RS rows. For
men's version, work WS buttonhole rows (in left
front) as folls: patt 2 sts, work 2 tog, yrn (to make
a buttonhole), patt to end. For lady's version, work
WS buttonhole rows (in right front) as folls: patt to
last 4 sts, yrn, work 2 tog (to make a buttonhole),
patt 2 sts.

BACK

Using 4mm (US 6) needles cast on 87 [93: 99: 105:
111: 115: 121: 127] sts.

Row 1 (RS): K1 [0: 1: 0: 1: 1: 0: 1], ★P1, K1, rep
from ★ to last 0 [1: 0: 1: 0: 0: 1: 0] st, P0 [1: 0: 1: 0:
0: 1: 0].

Row 2: As row 1.

These 2 rows form moss st.

Work in moss st for a further 9 rows, ending with
WS facing for next row.

Row 12 (WS): Moss st 15 [17: 17: 19: 21: 20: 22:
24] sts, ★M1, moss st 2 sts, M1, moss st 17 [17: 19:
19: 19: 21: 21: 21] sts, M1, moss st 2 sts, M1★, moss
st 15 [17: 19: 21: 23: 25: 27: 29] sts, rep from ★ to ★
once more, moss st 15 [17: 17: 19: 21: 20: 22: 24] sts.
95 [101: 107: 113: 119: 123: 129: 135] sts.

Change to 4½mm (US 7) needles.

Now work in patt as folls:

Row 1 (RS): K14 [16: 16: 18: 20: 19: 21: 23], ★P1,
K4, P1, K15 [15: 17: 17: 17: 19: 19: 19], P1, K4, P1★,
K13 [15: 17: 19: 21: 23: 25: 27], rep from ★ to ★ once
more, K14 [16: 16: 18: 20: 19: 21: 23].

Row 2: P14 [16: 16: 18: 20: 19: 21: 23], ★K1, P4, K1,
P15 [15: 17: 17: 17: 19: 19: 19], K1, P4, K1★, P13 [15:

48

17: 19: 21: 23: 25: 27], rep from ★ to ★ once more, P14 [16: 16: 18: 20: 19: 21: 23].

Row 3: K14 [16: 16: 18: 20: 19: 21: 23], *P1, C4B, P1, K15 [15: 17: 17: 17: 19: 19: 19], P1, C4F, P1★, K13 [15: 17: 19: 21: 23: 25: 27], rep from ★ to ★ once more, K14 [16: 16: 18: 20: 19: 21: 23].

Row 4: As row 2.

Rows 5 and 6: As rows 1 and 2.

These 6 rows form patt.

Keeping patt correct throughout, cont as folls:

Next row (RS): K1, M1, patt to last st, M1, K1.

97 [103: 109: 115: 121: 125: 131: 137] sts.

Working all side seam increases as set by last row, inc 1 st at each end of 12th [12th: 12th: 14th: 12th: 12th: 12th: 14th] and every foll 12th [12th: 14th: 14th: 14th: 14th: 12th: 14th] row to 105 [107: 119: 123: 131: 135: 135: 147] sts, then on every foll 14th [14th: -: 16th: -: -: 14th: -] row until there are 107 [113: -: 125: -: -: 141: -] sts.

Work 13 [13: 13: 15: 13: 13: 13: 15] rows, ending with RS facing for next row. (Back should meas approx 36.5 [38: 39: 41.5: 39: 39: 38: 40.5] cm.)

Shape armholes

Keeping patt correct, cast off 5 sts at beg of next 2 rows. 97 [103: 109: 115: 121: 125: 131: 137] sts.

Dec 1 st at each end of next 5 rows, then on foll 5 alt rows, ending with **WS** facing for next row.

77 [83: 89: 95: 101: 105: 111: 117] sts.

Next row (WS): P5 [7: 7: 9: 11: 10: 12: 14], *K1, (P2tog) twice, K1, P15 [15: 17: 17: 17: 19: 19: 19], K1, (P2tog tbl) twice, K1★, P13 [15: 17: 19: 21: 23: 25: 27], rep from ★ to ★ once more, P5 [7: 7: 9: 11: 10: 12: 14]. 69 [75: 81: 87: 93: 97: 103: 109] sts.

Work in g st for 4 rows, dec 1 st at each end of 3rd of these rows and ending with RS facing for next row. 67 [73: 79: 85: 91: 95: 101: 107] sts.

Beg with a K row, complete back in st st as folls:

Work 26 [30: 34: 36: 42: 46: 50: 52] rows, ending with RS facing for next row. (Armhole should meas approx 19 [20.5: 22: 23: 25.5: 27: 28.5: 29.5] cm.)

Shape back neck and shoulders

Next row (RS): K22 [25: 27: 30: 32: 34: 36: 39] and turn, leaving rem sts on a holder.

Work each side of neck separately.

Dec 1 st at neck edge of next 4 rows **and at same time** cast off 6 [7: 8: 9: 9: 10: 11: 12] sts at beg of

2nd and foll alt row.

Work 1 row.

Cast off rem 6 [7: 7: 8: 10: 10: 10: 11] sts.

With RS facing, slip centre 23 [23: 25: 25: 27: 27: 29: 29] sts onto a holder, rejoin yarn and K to end.

Complete to match first side, reversing shapings.

POCKET FLAPS (make 2)

Using 4mm (US 6) needles cast on 23 [23: 25: 25: 25: 27: 27: 27] sts.

Rows 1 to 3: Knit.

Change to 4½mm (US 7) needles.

Row 4 (WS): K2, P to last 2 sts, K2.

Row 5: Knit.

Rep last 2 rows 4 [4: 4: 5: 5: 5: 5: 5] times more, then row 4 again, ending with RS facing for next row.

Break yarn and leave sts on a holder.

LEFT FRONT

Using 4mm (US 6) needles cast on 49 [52: 55: 58: 61: 63: 66: 69] sts.

Row 1 (RS): K1 [0: 1: 0: 1: 1: 0: 1], *P1, K1, rep from ★ to end.

Row 2: (K1, P1) 3 times, K3, *P1, K1, rep from ★ to last 0 [1: 0: 1: 0: 0: 1: 0] st, P0 [1: 0: 1: 0: 0: 1: 0].

Row 3: K1 [0: 1: 0: 1: 1: 0: 1], *P1, K1, rep from ★ to last 8 sts, P2, (K1, P1) 3 times.

Row 4: (P1, K1) 3 times, P1, K2, *P1, K1, rep from ★ to last 0 [1: 0: 1: 0: 0: 1: 0] st, P0 [1: 0: 1: 0: 0: 1: 0].

These 4 rows set the sts − front opening edge 7 sts in double moss st, side edge sts in moss st and one st in rev st st between.

Lady's version only

Cont as set for a further 7 rows, ending with **WS** facing for next row.

Men's version only

Cont as set for a further 0 [0: 2: 2: 2: 2: 2: 0] rows, ending with RS facing for next row.

Next row (buttonhole row) (RS): Patt to last 4 sts, yrn, work 2 tog (to make a buttonhole), patt 2 sts.

Working a further 5 buttonholes in this way on every foll 23rd [25th: 25th: 27th: 27th: 27th: 27th: 29th] row, referring to pattern note for how to work buttonholes on WS rows and noting that no further reference will be made to buttonholes, cont as folls:

Work 6 [6: 4: 4: 4: 4: 4: 6] rows, ending with **WS** facing for next row.

Both versions

Row 12 (WS): Patt 13 [14: 15: 16: 17: 18: 19: 20] sts, M1, moss st 2 sts, M1, moss st 17 [17: 19: 19: 19: 21: 21: 21] sts, M1, moss st 2 sts, M1, moss st 15 [17: 17: 19: 21: 20: 22: 24] sts.

53 [56: 59: 62: 65: 67: 70: 73] sts.

Change to 4½mm (US 7) needles.

Now work in patt as folls:

Row 1 (RS): K14 [16: 16: 18: 20: 19: 21: 23], P1, K4, P1, K15 [15: 17: 17: 17: 19: 19: 19], P1, K4, P1, K4 [5: 6: 7: 8: 9: 10: 11], patt 8 sts.

Row 2: Patt 8 sts, P4 [5: 6: 7: 8: 9: 10: 11], K1, P4, K1, P15 [15: 17: 17: 17: 19: 19: 19], K1, P4, K1, P14 [16: 16: 18: 20: 19: 21: 23].

Row 3: K14 [16: 16: 18: 20: 19: 21: 23], P1, C4B, P1, K15 [15: 17: 17: 17: 19: 19: 19], P1, C4F, P1, K4 [5: 6: 7: 8: 9: 10: 11], patt 8 sts.

Row 4: As row 2.

Rows 5 and 6: As rows 1 and 2.

These 6 rows set the sts – front opening edge 7 sts in double moss st, one st in rev st st, and rem sts in cable patt.

Keeping patt correct throughout, cont as folls:

Working all side seam increases as set by back, inc 1 st at beg of next and every foll 12th [12th: 12th: 14th: 12th: 12th: 12th: 14th] row to 58 [59: 61: 67: 67: 69: 73: 79] sts, then on every foll 14th [14th: 14th: 16th: 14th: 14th: 14th: -] row until there are 59 [62: 65: 68: 71: 73: 76: -] sts.

Work 13 [13: 13: 15: 13: 13: 13: 15] rows, ending with RS facing for next row.

Shape armhole

Keeping patt correct, cast off 5 sts at beg of next row. 54 [57: 60: 63: 66: 68: 71: 74] sts.

Work 1 row.

Dec 1 st at armhole edge of next 5 rows, then on foll 5 alt rows, ending with **WS** facing for next row. 44 [47: 50: 53: 56: 58: 61: 64] sts.

Next row (WS): Patt 12 [13: 14: 15: 16: 17: 18: 19] sts, K1, (P2tog) twice, K1, P15 [15: 17: 17: 17: 19: 19: 19], K1, (P2tog tbl) twice, K1, P5 [7: 7: 9: 11: 10: 12: 14]. 40 [43: 46: 49: 52: 54: 57: 60] sts.

Place pocket flap

Next row (RS): K5 [7: 7: 9: 11: 10: 12: 14], holding

WS of first pocket flap against RS of left front K tog first st of flap with next st of front, (K tog next st of flap with next st of front) 22 [22: 24: 24: 24: 26: 26: 26] times, K4 [5: 6: 7: 8: 9: 10: 11], patt 8 sts.

Next row: Patt 8 sts, K to end.

Next row: K2tog, K to last 8 sts, patt 8 sts. 39 [42: 45: 48: 51: 53: 56: 59] sts.

Next row: Patt 8 sts, K to end.

Next row (RS): K to last 8 sts, patt 8 sts.

Next row: Patt 8 sts, P to end.

Last 2 rows set the sts for rest of left front – front opening edge 8 sts still in patt as set, and all other sts now in st st.

Keeping sts correct as now set, cont as folls:

Work 8 [12: 16: 18: 22: 26: 28: 30] rows, ending with RS facing for next row.

Shape front neck

Next row (RS): K28 [31: 33: 36: 39: 41: 44: 47] and turn, leaving rem 11 [11: 12: 12: 12: 12: 12: 12] sts on a holder (for collar).

Dec 1 st at neck edge of next 6 rows, then on foll 3 [3: 3: 3: 4: 4: 5: 5] alt rows, then on foll 4th row. 18 [21: 23: 26: 28: 30: 32: 35] sts.

Work 1 row, ending with RS facing for next row.

Shape shoulder

Cast off 6 [7: 8: 9: 9: 10: 11: 12] sts at beg of next and foll alt row.

Work 1 row.

Cast off rem 6 [7: 7: 8: 10: 10: 10: 11] sts.

RIGHT FRONT

Using 4mm (US 6) needles cast on 49 [52: 55: 58: 61: 63: 66: 69] sts.

Row 1 (RS): *K1, P1, rep from * to last 1 [0: 1: 0: 1: 1: 0: 1] st, K1 [0: 1: 0: 1: 1: 0: 1].

Row 2: P0 [1: 0: 1: 0: 0: 1: 0], *K1, P1, rep from * to last 9 sts, K3, (P1, K1) 3 times.

Row 3: (P1, K1) 3 times, P2, *K1, P1, rep from * to last 1 [0: 1: 0: 1: 1: 0: 1] st, K1 [0: 1: 0: 1: 1: 0: 1].

Row 4: P0 [1: 0: 1: 0: 0: 1: 0], *K1, P1, rep from * to last 9 sts, K2, P1, (K1, P1) 3 times.

These 4 rows set the sts – front opening edge 7 sts in double moss st, side edge sts in moss st and one st in rev st st between.

Lady's version only

Cont as set for a further 0 [0: 2: 2: 2: 2: 2: 0] rows,

ending with RS facing for next row.

Next row (buttonhole row) (RS): Patt 2 sts, work 2 tog, yrn (to make a buttonhole), patt to end. Working a further 5 buttonholes in this way on every foll 23rd [25th: 25th: 27th: 27th: 27th: 27th: 29th] row, referring to pattern note for how to work buttonholes on WS rows and noting that no further reference will be made to buttonholes, cont as folls: Work 6 [6: 4: 4: 4: 4: 4: 6] rows, ending with **WS** facing for next row.

Men's version only

Cont as set for a further 7 rows, ending with **WS** facing for next row.

Both versions

Row 12 (WS): Moss st 15 [17: 17: 19: 21: 20: 22: 24] sts, M1, moss st 2 sts, M1, moss st 17 [17: 19: 19: 19: 21: 21: 21] sts, M1, moss st 2 sts, M1, patt 13 [14: 15: 16: 17: 18: 19: 20] sts.
53 [56: 59: 62: 65: 67: 70: 73] sts.
Change to 4½mm (US 7) needles.
Now work in patt as folls:

Row 1 (RS): Patt 8 sts, K4 [5: 6: 7: 8: 9: 10: 11], P1, K4, P1, K15 [15: 17: 17: 17: 19: 19: 19], P1, K4, P1, K14 [16: 16: 18: 20: 19: 21: 23].

Row 2: P14 [16: 16: 18: 20: 19: 21: 23], K1, P4, K1, P15 [15: 17: 17: 17: 19: 19: 19], K1, P4, K1, P4 [5: 6: 7: 8: 9: 10: 11], patt 8 sts.

Row 3: Patt 8 sts, K4 [5: 6: 7: 8: 9: 10: 11], P1, C4B, P1, K15 [15: 17: 17: 17: 19: 19: 19], P1, C4F, P1, K14 [16: 16: 18: 20: 19: 21: 23].

Row 4: As row 2.

Rows 5 and 6: As rows 1 and 2.

These 6 rows set the sts – front opening edge 7 sts in double moss st, one st in rev st st, and rem sts in cable patt.

Keeping patt correct throughout, cont as folls:
Working all side seam increases as set by back, inc 1 st at end of next and every foll 12th [12th: 12th: 14th: 12th: 12th: 12th: 14th] row to 58 [59: 61: 67: 67: 69: 73: 79] sts, then on every foll 14th [14th: 14th: 16th: 14th: 14th: 14th: -] row until there are 59 [62: 65: 68: 71: 73: 76: -] sts.
Work 13 [13: 13: 15: 13: 13: 13: 15] rows, ending with RS facing for next row.

Shape armhole

Work 1 row.

Keeping patt correct, cast off 5 sts at beg of next row. 54 [57: 60: 63: 66: 68: 71: 74] sts.
Dec 1 st at armhole edge of next 5 rows, then on foll 5 alt rows, ending with **WS** facing for next row. 44 [47: 50: 53: 56: 58: 61: 64] sts.

Next row (WS): P5 [7: 7: 9: 11: 10: 12: 14], K1, (P2tog) twice, K1, P15 [15: 17: 17: 17: 19: 19: 19], K1, (P2tog tbl) twice, K1, patt 12 [13: 14: 15: 16: 17: 18: 19] sts. 40 [43: 46: 49: 52: 54: 57: 60] sts.

Place pocket flap

Next row (RS): Patt 8 sts, K4 [5: 6: 7: 8: 9: 10: 11], holding WS of second pocket flap against RS of right front K tog first st of flap with next st of front, (K tog next st of flap with next st of front) 22 [22: 24: 24: 24: 26: 26: 26] times, K5 [7: 7: 9: 11: 10: 12: 14].

Next row: K to last 8 sts, patt 8 sts.

Next row: Patt 8 sts, K to last 2 sts, K2tog. 39 [42: 45: 48: 51: 53: 56: 59] sts.

Next row: K to last 8 sts, patt 8 sts.

Next row (RS): Patt 8 sts, K to end.

Next row: P to last 8 sts, patt 8 sts.

Last 2 rows set the sts for rest of right front – front opening edge 8 sts still in patt as set, and all other sts now in st st.
Keeping sts correct as now set, cont as folls:
Work 8 [12: 16: 18: 22: 26: 28: 30] rows, ending with RS facing for next row.

Shape front neck

Next row (RS): Patt 11 [11: 12: 12: 12: 12: 12: 12] sts and slip these sts onto a holder (for collar), K to end. 28 [31: 33: 36: 39: 41: 44: 47] sts.
Complete to match left front, reversing shapings.

SLEEVES

Using 4mm (US 6) needles cast on 45 [47: 49: 51: 51: 53: 53: 55] sts.
Work in moss st as given for back for 12 rows, ending with RS facing for next row.
Change to 4½mm (US 7) needles.
Beg with a K row and working all sleeve increases in same way as side seam increases, work in st st, shaping sides by inc 1 st at each end of 3rd [5th: 5th: 5th: 5th: 3rd: 3rd: 3rd] and every foll 4th [6th: 6th: 6th: 6th: 4th: 4th: 4th] row to 53 [79: 81: 79: 89: 57: 63: 63] sts, then on every foll 6th [-: 8th: 8th: -:

6th: 6th: 6th] row until there are 77 [-: 83: 85: -: 93: 95: 97] sts.

Cont straight until sleeve meas 44 [47: 50: 52: 54: 55: 55: 56] cm, ending with RS facing for next row.

Shape top

Cast off 5 sts at beg of next 2 rows.

67 [69: 73: 75: 79: 83: 85: 87] sts.

Dec 1 st at each end of next 5 rows, then on every foll alt row until 37 sts rem, then on foll 9 rows, ending with RS facing for next row.

Cast off rem 19 sts.

MAKING UP

Press as described on the information page.

Join both shoulder seams using back stitch, or mattress stitch if preferred.

Collar

With RS facing and using 4mm (US 6) needles, slip 11 [11: 12: 12: 12: 12: 12: 12] sts from right front holder onto right needle, rejoin yarn and pick up and knit 18 [18: 18: 18: 20: 20: 22: 22] sts up right side of front neck, and 5 sts down right side of back neck, K across 23 [23: 25: 25: 27: 27: 29: 29] sts on back holder, then pick up and knit 5 sts up left side of back neck, and 18 [18: 18: 18: 20: 20: 22: 22] sts down left side of front neck, then patt across 11 [11: 12: 12: 12: 12: 12: 12] sts on left front holder.

91 [91: 95: 95: 101: 101: 107: 107] sts.

Working all sts in double moss st as set by front opening edge sts, cont as folls:

Cast off 4 sts at beg of next 2 rows.

83 [83: 87: 87: 93: 93: 99: 99] sts.

Next row (RS of collar, WS of body): Patt 6 [6: 8: 8: 6: 6: 9: 9] sts, inc twice in next st, (patt 9 sts, inc twice in next st) 7 [7: 7: 7: 8: 8: 8: 8] times, patt 6 [6: 8: 8: 6: 6: 9: 9] sts. 99 [99: 103: 103: 111: 111: 117: 117] sts.

Working all increased sts in double moss st as set, cont straight until collar meas 9 cm from pick-up row, ending with RS of collar facing for next row.

Cast off in patt.

See information page for finishing instructions, setting in sleeves using the set-in method.

Using photograph as a guide, sew 2 buttons onto each pocket flap to secure flaps to fronts.

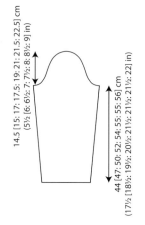

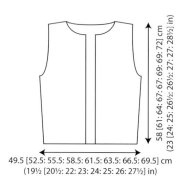

14.5 [15: 17: 17.5: 19: 21: 21.5: 22.5] cm
(5½ [6: 6½: 7: 7½: 8: 8½: 9] in)

44 [47: 50: 52: 54: 55: 55: 56] cm
(17½ [18½: 19½: 20½: 21½: 21½: 21½: 22] in)

58 [61: 64: 67: 67: 69: 69: 72] cm
(23 [24: 25: 26½: 26½: 27: 27: 28½] in)

49.5 [52.5: 55.5: 58.5: 61.5: 63.5: 66.5: 69.5] cm
(19½ [20½: 22: 23: 24: 25: 26: 27½] in)

Information

Tension

Obtaining the correct tension is perhaps the single factor which can make the difference between a successful garment and a disastrous one. It controls both the shape and size of an article, so any variation, however slight, can distort the finished garment. Different designers feature in our books and it is their tension, given at the start of each pattern, which you must match. We recommend that you knit a square in pattern and/or stocking stitch (depending on the pattern instructions) of perhaps 5 - 10 more stitches and 5 - 10 more rows than those given in the tension note. Mark out the central 10cm square with pins. If you have too many stitches to 10cm try again using thicker needles, if you have too few stitches to 10cm try again using finer needles. Once you have achieved the correct tension your garment will be knitted to the measurements indicated in the size diagram shown at the end of the pattern.

Chart Note

Many of the patterns in the book are worked from charts. Each square on a chart represents a stitch and each line of squares a row of knitting. Each colour used is given a different letter and these are shown in the materials section, or in the key alongside the chart of each pattern. When working from the charts, read odd rows (K) from right to left and even rows (P) from left to right, unless otherwise stated. When working lace from a chart it is important to note that all but the largest size may have to alter the first and last few stitches in order not to lose or gain stitches over the row.

Working A Lace Pattern

When working a lace pattern it is important to remember that if you are unable to work both the increase and corresponding decrease and vica versa, the stitches should be worked in stocking stitch.

Knitting With Colour

There are two main methods of working colour into a knitted fabric: **Intarsia** and **Fairisle** techniques. The first method produces a single thickness of fabric and is usually used where a colour is only required in a particular area of a row and does not form a repeating pattern across the row, as in the fairisle technique.

Fairisle type knitting: When two or three colours are worked repeatedly across a row, strand the yarn not in use loosely behind the stitches being worked. If you are working with more than two colours, treat the "floating" yarns as if they were one yarn and always spread the stitches to their correct width to keep them elastic. It is advisable not to carry the stranded or "floating" yarns over more than three stitches at a time, but to weave them under and over the colour you are working. The "floating" yarns are therefore caught at the back of the work.

Intarsia: The simplest way to do this is to cut short lengths of yarn for each motif or block of colour used in a row. Then joining in the various colours at the appropriate point on the row, link one colour to the next by twisting them around each other where they meet on the wrong side to avoid gaps. All ends can then either be darned along the colour join lines, as each motif is completed or then can be "knitted-in" to the fabric of the knitting as each colour is worked into the pattern. This is done in much the same way as "weaving- in" yarns when working the Fairisle technique and does save time darning-in ends. It is essential that the tension is noted for intarsia as this may vary from the stocking stitch if both are used in the same pattern.

Finishing Instructions

After working for hours knitting a garment, it seems a great pity that many garments are spoiled because such little care is taken in the pressing and finishing process. Follow the text below for a truly professional-looking garment.

Pressing

Block out each piece of knitting and following the instructions on the ball band press the garment pieces, omitting the ribs. Tip: Take special care to press the edges, as this will make sewing up both easier and neater. If the ball band indicates that the fabric is not to be pressed, then covering the blocked out fabric with a damp white cotton cloth and leaving it to stand will have the desired effect. Darn in all ends neatly along the selvage edge or a colour join, as appropriate.

Stitching

When stitching the pieces together, remember to match areas of colour and texture very carefully where they meet. Use a seam stitch such as back stitch or mattress stitch for all main knitting seams and join all ribs and neckband with mattress stitch, unless otherwise stated.

Construction

Having completed the pattern instructions, join left shoulder and neckband seams as detailed above. Sew the top of the sleeve to the body of the garment using the method detailed in the pattern, referring to the appropriate guide:

Straight cast-off sleeves: Place centre of cast-off edge of sleeve to shoulder seam. Sew top of sleeve to body, using markers as guidelines where applicable.

Square set-in sleeves: Place centre of cast-off edge of sleeve to shoulder seam. Set sleeve head into armhole, the straight sides at top of sleeve to form a neat right-angle to cast-off sts at armhole on back and front.

Shallow set-in sleeves: Place centre of cast off edge of sleeve to shoulder seam. Match decreases at beg of armhole shaping to decreases at top of sleeve. Sew sleeve head into armhole, easing in shapings.

Set-in sleeves: Place centre of cast-off edge of sleeve to shoulder seam. Set in sleeve, easing sleeve head into armhole. Join side and sleeve seams.

Slip stitch pocket edgings and linings into place.

Sew on buttons to correspond with buttonholes.

Ribbed welts and neckbands and any areas of garter stitch should not be pressed.

Information

Abbreviations

K	knit
P	purl
st(s)	stitch(es)
inc	increas(e)(ing)
dec	decreas(e)(ing)
st st	stocking stitch (1 row K, 1 row P)
g st	garter stitch (K every row)
beg	begin(ning)
foll	following
rem	remain(ing)
rev st st	reverse stocking stitch (1 row P , 1 row K)
rep	repeat
alt	alternate
cont	continue
patt	pattern
tog	together
mm	millimetres
cm	centimetres
in(s)	inch(es)
RS	right side
WS	wrong side
sl 1	slip one stitch
psso	pass slipped stitch over
p2sso	pass 2 slipped stitches over
tbl	through back of loop
M1	make one stitch by picking up horizontal loop before next stitch and knitting into back of it
M1P	make one stitch by picking up horizontal loop before next stitch and purling into back of it
yfwd	yarn forward
yrn	yarn round needle
meas	measures
0	no stitches, times or rows
–	no stitches, times or rows for that size
yo	yarn over needle
yfrn	yarn forward round needle
wyib	with yarn at back
sl2togK	slip 2 stitches together knitways

Crochet Terms

UK crochet terms and abbreviations have been used throughout. The list below gives the US equivalent where they vary.

ABBREV.	UK	US
dc (sc)	double crochet	(single crochet)
htr (hdc)	half treble	(half double crochet)
tr (dc)	treble	(double crochet)
dtr (tr)	double treble	(treble)

Experience Rating
For guidance only

★

Easy, straight forward knitting

★ ★

For the more experienced knitter

★ ★ ★

Advanced techniques used

Buttons and ribbons used in this magazine are sourced from:

Coats Crafts UK, Green Lane Mill, Holmfirth,
West Yorkshire HD9 2DX.
www.knitrowan.com
www.coatscrafts.co.uk
Tel: +44 (0)1484 681881
Email: mail@knitrowan.com

Bedecked Haberdashery,
Willow Cottage Workshop,
New Radnor,
Presteigne,
Powys,
LD8 2SS
www.bedecked.co.uk
Shop tel: 01544 350577
Email: thegirls@bedecked.co.uk

Rowan recommends MILWARD haberdashery products

Wash Care Information

You may have noticed over the last season that the wash care symbols on our ball bands and shade cards have changed. This is to bring the symbols we use up to date and hopefully help you to care for your knitting and crochet more easily. Below are the symbols you are likely to see and a brief explanation of each.

MACHINE WASH SYMBOLS

Machine Wash, Cold   Machine Wash, Cold, Gentle   Machine Wash, Warm   Machine Wash, Warm, Gentle

HAND WASH SYMBOLS

Do Not Wash   Hand Wash, Normal   Hand Wash, Cold   Hand Wash, Warm

DRY CLEAN SYMBOLS

Do Not Dry Clean   Dry Clean   Dry Clean, in Certain Solvents, Consult Cleaner   Dry Clean, Any Solvent

IRONING SYMBOLS

Do Not Iron   Iron Low Heat   Iron Medium Heat

DO NOT BLEACH SYMBOL

Do Not Bleach

DRYING SYMBOLS

Do Not Tumble Dry   Tumble Dry, Gentle, Low Heat   Dry Flat in Shade

Do Not Wring

Sizing Guide

When you knit and wear a Rowan design we want you to look and feel fabulous. This all starts with the size and fit of the design you choose. To help you to achieve a great knitting experience we have looked at the sizing of our womens and menswear patterns. This has resulted in the introduction of our new sizing guide which includes the following exciting features:

Our sizing now conforms to standard clothing sizes. Therefore if you buy a standard size 12 in clothing, then our medium patterns will fit you perfectly.

The menswear designs are now available to knit in menswear sizes XSmall through to 2XL ie. 38" to 50" chest.

Dimensions in the charts below are body measurements, not garment dimensions, therefore please refer to the measuring guide to help you to determine which is the best size for you to knit.

STANDARD SIZING GUIDE FOR WOMEN

The sizing within this chart is also based on the larger size within the range, ie. M will be based on size 14

UK SIZE	S	M	L	XL	XXL	
DUAL SIZE	8/10	12/14	16/18	20/22	24/26	
To fit bust	32 – 34	36 – 38	40 – 42	44 – 46	48 – 50	inches
	81 – 86	91 - 97	102 – 107	112 – 117	122 – 127	cm
To fit waist	24 – 26	28 – 30	32 – 34	36 – 38	40 – 42	inches
	61 – 66	71 – 76	81 – 86	91 – 97	102 – 107	cm
To fit hips	34 – 36	38 – 40	42 – 44	46 – 48	50 – 52	inches

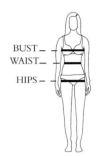

BUST
WAIST

HIPS

STANDARD MENS SIZING GUIDE

Mens sizes: XS to 2XL. Unisex Sizes: XXS to 2XL

UK SIZE	XXS	XS	S	M	L	XL	XXL	2XL	
EUR Size	46	48	50	52	54	56	58	60	
To fit chest	36	38	40	42	44	46	48	50	inches
	91	97	102	107	112	117	122	127	cm
To fit waist	28	30	32	34	36	36	40	42	inches
	71	76	81	86	91	97	102	107	cms

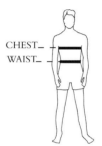

CHEST
WAIST

SIZING & SIZE DIAGRAM NOTE

The instructions are given for the smallest size. Where they vary, work the figures in brackets for the larger sizes. **One set of figures refers to all sizes.** Included with most patterns in this magazine is a **'size diagram'** - see image on the right, of the finished garment and its dimensions. The measurement shown at the bottom of each **'size diagram'** shows the garment width 2.5cm below the armhole shaping. To help you choose the size of garment to knit please refer to the sizing guide. Generally in the majority of designs the welt width (at the cast on edge of the garment) is the same width as the chest. However, some designs are 'A-Line' in shape or flared edge and in these cases welt width will be wider than the chest width.

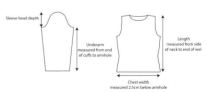

Sleeve head depth

Underarm measured from end of cuffs to armhole

Length measured from side of neck to end of welt

Chest width measured 2.5cm below armhole

MEASURING GUIDE

For maximum comfort and to ensure the correct fit when choosing a size to knit, please follow the tips below when checking your size. Measure yourself close to your body, over your underwear and don't pull the tape measure too tight!

Bust/chest – measure around the fullest part of the bust/chest and across the shoulder blades.

Waist – measure around the natural waistline, just above the hip bone.

Hips – measure around the fullest part of the bottom.

If you don't wish to measure yourself, note the size of a favourite jumper that you like the fit of. Our sizes are now comparable to the clothing sizes from the major high street retailers, so if your favourite jumper is a size Medium or size 12, then our casual size Medium and standard size 12 should be approximately the same fit.

To be extra sure, measure your favourite jumper and then compare these measurements with the Rowan size diagram given at the end of the individual instructions.

Finally, once you have decided which size is best for you, please ensure that you achieve the tension required for the design you wish to knit. Remember if your tension is too loose, your garment will be bigger than the pattern size and you may use more yarn. If your tension is too tight, your garment could be smaller than the pattern size and you will have yarn left over.

Furthermore if your tension is incorrect, the handle of your fabric will be too stiff or floppy and will not fit properly. It really does make sense to check your tension before starting every project.

Stockist

AUSTRALIA: Australian Country Spinners, Pty Ltd, Level 7, 409 St. Kilda Road, Melbourne Vic 3004.
Tel: 03 9380 3888   Fax: 03 9820 0989   Email: customerservice@auspinners.com.au

AUSTRIA: Coats Harlander Ges.m.b.H.., Autokaderstraße 29, 1210 Wien, Austria
Tel: 00800 26 27 28 00   Fax: (00) 49 7644 802-133
Email: coats.harlander@coats.com   Web: www.coatscrafts.at

BELGIUM: Coats N.V., c/o Coats GmbH Kaiserstr.1 79341 Kenzingen Germany
Tel: 0032 (0) 800 77 89 2   Fax: 00 49 7644 802 133   Email: sales.coatsninove@coats.com
Web: www.coatscrafts.be

BULGARIA: Coats Bulgaria, 7 Magnaurska Shkola Str., BG-1784 Sofia, Bulgaria
Tel: (+359 2) 976 77 41   Fax: (+359 2) 976 77 20   Email: officebg@coats.com
Web: www.coatsbulgaria.bg

CANADA: Westminster Fibers, 10 Roybridge Gate, Suite 200, Vaughan, Ontario L4H 3M8
Tel: (800) 263-2354   Fax: 905-856-6184   Email: info@westminsterfibers.com

CHINA: Coats Shanghai Ltd, No 9 Building , Baosheng Road, Songjiang Industrial Zone, Shanghai.
Tel: (86- 21) 13816681825   Fax: (86-21) 57743733-326   Email: victor.li@coats.com

CYPRUS: Coats Bulgaria, 7 Magnaurska Shkola Str., BG-1784 Sofia, Bulgaria
Tel: (+359 2) 976 77 41   Fax: (+359 2) 976 77 20   Email: officebg@coats.com
Web: www.coatscrafts.com.cy

CZECH REPUBLIC: Coats Czecho s.r.o.Staré Mesto 246 569 32
Tel: (420) 461616633   Email: galanterie@coats.com

ESTONIA: Coats Eesti AS, Ampri tee 9/4, 74001 Viimsi Harjumaa
Tel: +372 630 6250   Fax: +372 630 6260   Email: info@coats.ee   Web: www.coatscrafts.co.ee

DENMARK: Carl J. Permin A/S Egegaardsvej 28 DK-2610 Rødovre
Tel: (45) 36 72 12 00   E-mail: permin@permin.dk

FINLAND: Coats Opti Crafts Oy, Huhtimontie 6 04200 KERAVA
Tel: (358) 9 274871   Email: coatsopti.sales@coats.com   www.coatscrafts.fi

FRANCE: Coats France, c/o Coats GmbH, Kaiserstr.1, 79341 Kenzingen, Germany
Tel: (0) 0810 06 00 02   Email: artsdufil@coats.com   Web: www.coatscrafts.fr

GERMANY: Coats GmbH, Kaiserstr. 1, 79341 Kenzingen, Germany
Tel: 0049 7644 802 222   Email: kenzingen.vertrieb@coats.com   Fax: 0049 7644 802 300
Web: www.coatsgmbh.de

GREECE: Coats Bulgaria, 7 Magnaurska Shkola Str., BG-1784 Sofia, Bulgaria
Tel: (+359 2) 976 77 41   Fax: (+359 2) 976 77 20   Email: officebg@coats.com
Web: www.coatscrafts.gr

HOLLAND: Coats B.V., c/o Coats GmbH, Kaiserstr.1, 79341 Kenzingen, Germany
Tel: 0031 (0) 800 02 26 6488   Fax: 00 49 7644 802 133   Email: sales.coatsninove@coats.com
Web: www.coatscrafts.be

HONG KONG: East Unity Company Ltd, Unit B2, 7/F., Block B, Kailey Industrial Centre, 12 Fung Yip Street, Chai Wan
Tel: (852)2869 7110   Email: eastunityco@yahoo.com.hk

ICELAND: Storkurinn, Laugavegi 59, 101 Reykjavik
Tel: (354) 551 8258   Email: storkurinn@simnet.is

ITALY: Coats Cucirini srl, Viale Sarca no 223, 20126 Milano
Tel: 02636151   Fax: 0266111701

KOREA: Coats Korea Co. Ltd, 5F Eyeon B/D, 935-40 Bangbae-Dong, 137-060
Tel: (82) 2 521 6262   Fax: (82) 2 521 5181   Email: rozenpark@coats.com

LATVIA: Coats Latvija SIA, Mukusalas str. 41 b, Riga LV-1004
Tel: +371 67 625173   Fax: +371 67 892758   Email: info.latvia@coats.com
Web: www.coatscrafts.lv

LEBANON: y.knot, Saifi Village, Mkhalissiya Street 162, Beirut
Tel: (961) 1 992211   Fax: (961) 1 315553   Email: y.knot@cyberia.net.lb

LITHUANIA & RUSSIA: Coats Lietuva UAB, A. Juozapaviciaus str. 6/2, LT-09310 Vilnius
Tel: +370 527 30971   Fax: +370 527 2305   Email: info@coats.lt
Web: www.coatscrafts.lt

LUXEMBOURG: Coats N.V., c/o Coats GmbH, Kaiserstr.1, 79341 Kenzingen, Germany
Tel: 00 49 7644 802 222   Fax: 00 49 7644 802 133   Email: sales.coatsninove@coats.com
Web: www.coatscrafts.be

MALTA: John Gregory Ltd, 8 Ta'Xbiex Sea Front, Msida MSD 1512, Malta
Tel: +356 2133 0202   Fax: +356 2134 4745   Email: raygreg@onvol.net

MEXICO: Estambres Crochet SA de CV, Aaron Saenz 1891-7, PO Box SANTAMARIA, 64650 MONTERREY
TEL +52 (81) 8335-3870

NEW ZEALAND: ACS New Zealand, P.O Box 76199, Northwood, Christchurch New Zealand
Tel: 64 3 323 6665   Fax: 64 3 323 6660   Email: lynn@impactmg.co.nz

NORWAY: Falk Knappehuset AS, Svinesundsveien 347, 1788 Halden, Norway
Tel: +47 555 393 00   Email: post@falkgruppen.no

PORTUGAL: Coats & Clark, Quinta de Cravel, Apartado 444, 4431-968 Portugal
Tel: 00 351 223 770700

SINGAPORE: Golden Dragon Store, 101 Upper Cross Street #02-51, People's Park Centre, Singapore 058357
Tel: (65) 6 5358454   Fax: (65) 6 2216278   Email: gdscraft@hotmail.com

SLOVAKIA: Coats s.r.o.Kopcianska 94851 01 Bratislava
Tel: (421) 263532314   Email: galanteria@coats.com

SOUTH AFRICA: Arthur Bales LTD, 62 4th Avenue, Linden 2195
Tel: (27) 11 888 2401   Fax: (27) 11 782 6137   Email: arthurb@new.co.za

SPAIN: Coats Fabra SAU, Avda Meridiana 350, pta 13, 08027 Barcelona
Tel: (34) 932908400   Fax: 932908409   Email: atencion.clientes@coats.com

SWEDEN: Sweden Falkgruppen Stationsvägen 2, 516 31 Dalsjöfors, Sweden
Tel: +46(0)40 608 40 02   Email: kundtjanst@falk.se

SWITZERLAND: Coats Stroppel AG, Stroppelstrasse 20, 5417 Untersiggenthal, Switzerland
Tel: 00800 2627 2800   Fax: 0049 7644 802 133   Email: coats.stroppel@coats.com
Web: www.coatscrafts.ch

TAIWAN: Cactus Quality Co Ltd, 7FL-2, No. 140, Sec.2 Roosevelt R.d, Taipei, 10084 Taiwan, R.O.C.
Tel: 00886-2-23656527   Fax: 886-2-23656503   Email: cqcl@ms17.hinet.net

THAILAND: Global Wide Trading, 10 Lad Prao Soi 88, Bangkok 10310
Tel: 00 662 933 9019   Fax: 00 662 933 9110   Email: global.wide@yahoo.com

U.S.A.: Westminster Fibers, 8 Shelter Drive, Greer, South Carolina, 29650
Tel: (800) 445-9276   Fax: 864-879-9432   Email: info@westminsterfibers.com

U.K: Rowan, Green Lane Mill, Holmfirth, West Yorkshire, England HD9 2DX
Tel: +44 (0) 1484 681881   Fax: +44 (0) 1484 687920   Email: ccuk.sales@coats.com
Web: www.knitrowan.com

For stockists in all other countries please contact Rowan for details

Notes

Alba
Pattern page 25

Kerrera
Pattern page 27

Morna
Pattern page 32

Paisley
Pattern page 37

Sandrift Scarf
Pattern page 40

Skerry Beret
Pattern page 42

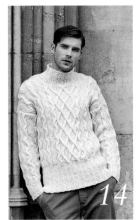

Spence
Pattern page 43

Spence
Pattern page 43

Tulloch Mens
Pattern page 48

Tulloch Womens
Pattern page 48